In the Spirit of Leadership | *A Vision Into A Different Future*

Cheryl Esposito

Copyright ©2008 by Cheryl Esposito

First Edition, 2008

Published in the United States of America by Plumb Road Publishing

Printed in Korea

Design and Production: The Graphics People – Susan Ellen Hogan, Mary Gilliana

ISBN 978-0-9799252-0-7

Library of Congress Control Number: 2007940519

Dedication

I dedicate this book to
Mark Stevenson,
the love of my life,
my husband, partner,
and best friend,
who makes all things possible.

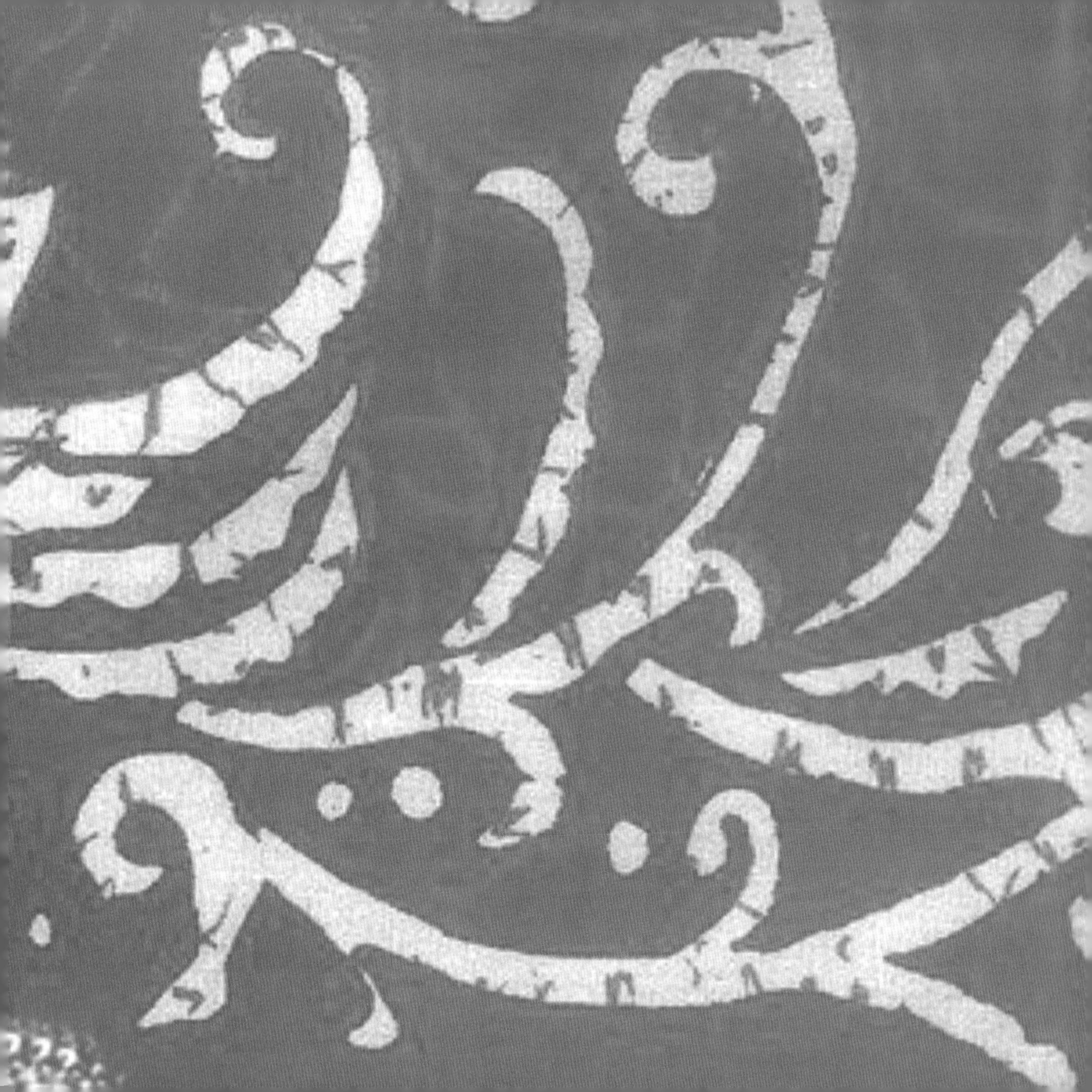

Table of Contents

Acknowledgements

It is a gift to feel gratitude. That means I have been blessed with experiences, relationships, moments that have made a difference in my life. In this moment, I am remembering how I got to this point. All the time that occurred before I ever had a conscious thought about my voice in print. All the encouragement I was given to write, long before I was willing. My writing coach Nancy Shanteau, with her patience, laser-like coaching and intuitive knowing, the writing took shape. The friends and family who kept asking, "how's the book coming along?" My spiritual teacher John Milton, who kept saying, "the book will come when it's ready."

If you are holding this book in your hands, and you had some part in its creation, this acknowledgement is for you. We do this for each other all the time, and it's not always visible. This book and Center for World Leadership are symbols of what happens when one person stands up and decides their voice matters.

What matters to you?

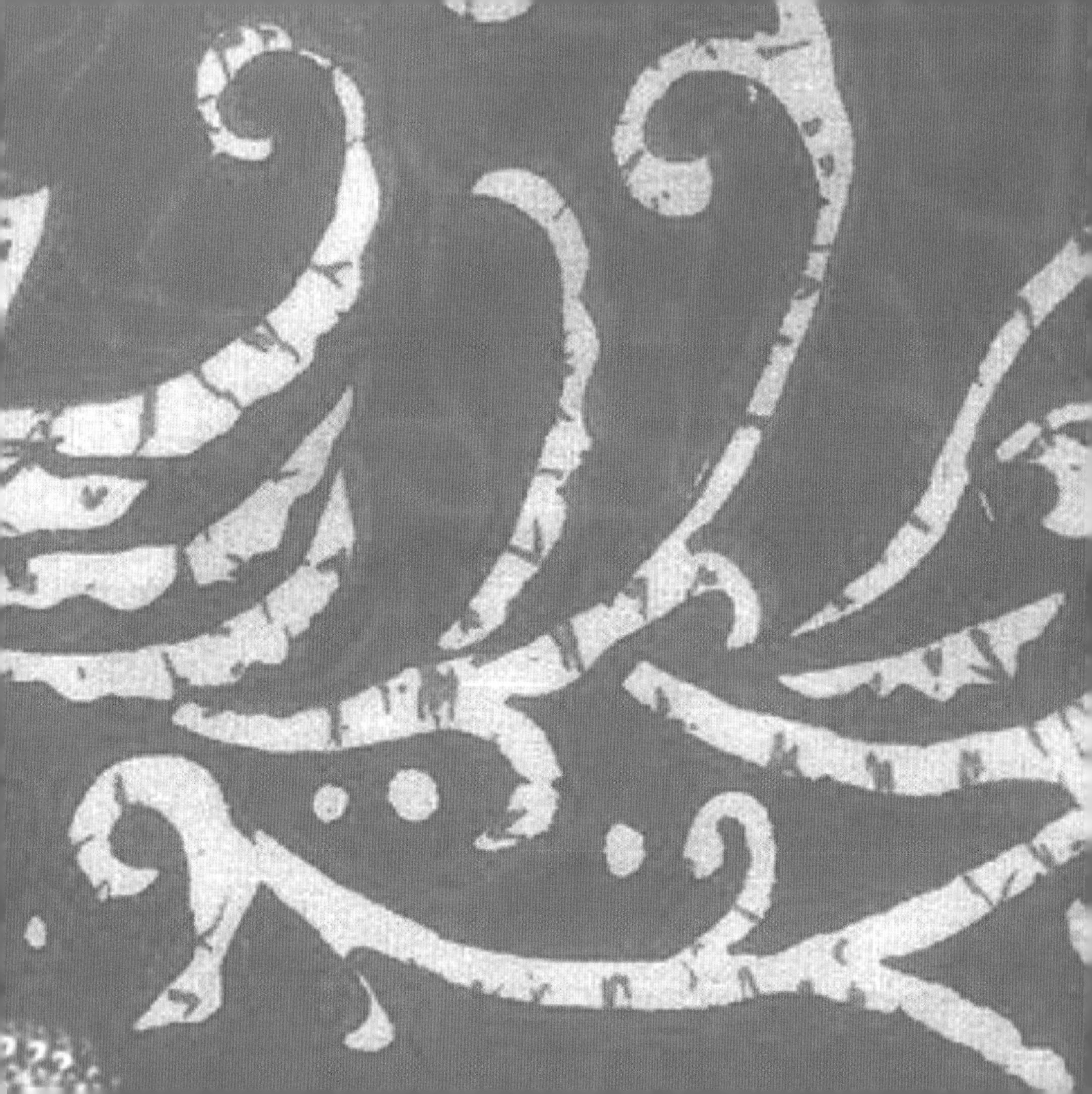

Introduction

The leadership journey is filled with tales of actions, successes, major growth of organizations, missteps in strategy. This book is the back story…what's happening along the way. The inner work we rarely hear about. The work that happens in the heart.

This book is for you:

- ❧ leaders who want something more, to step into a bigger vision or onto a different path in life
- ❧ coaches who want to see through, to find the thread, to touch that place in someone that is the opening
- ❧ anyone who feels a call to stepping out – or stepping in – to make a difference in the world

This book is for anyone who wants to share their voice or whose voice is coming out in a way that is taking unexpected shapes. My hope is that these poems and questions will encourage you; you don't have to fit yourself into someone else's box. Your words matter.

In the Spirit of Leadership | A Vision Into A Different Future

A Vision Into A Different Future

My work is about essence: the essence of a person, their spirit, their core, the self often hidden from view. In my executive coaching practice, I coach leaders who say they want to be more effective at what they do and have more meaning in their work, who want to be present with their family, and intentional in their lives as a whole.

Leadership is an invitation. What does your leadership invite?

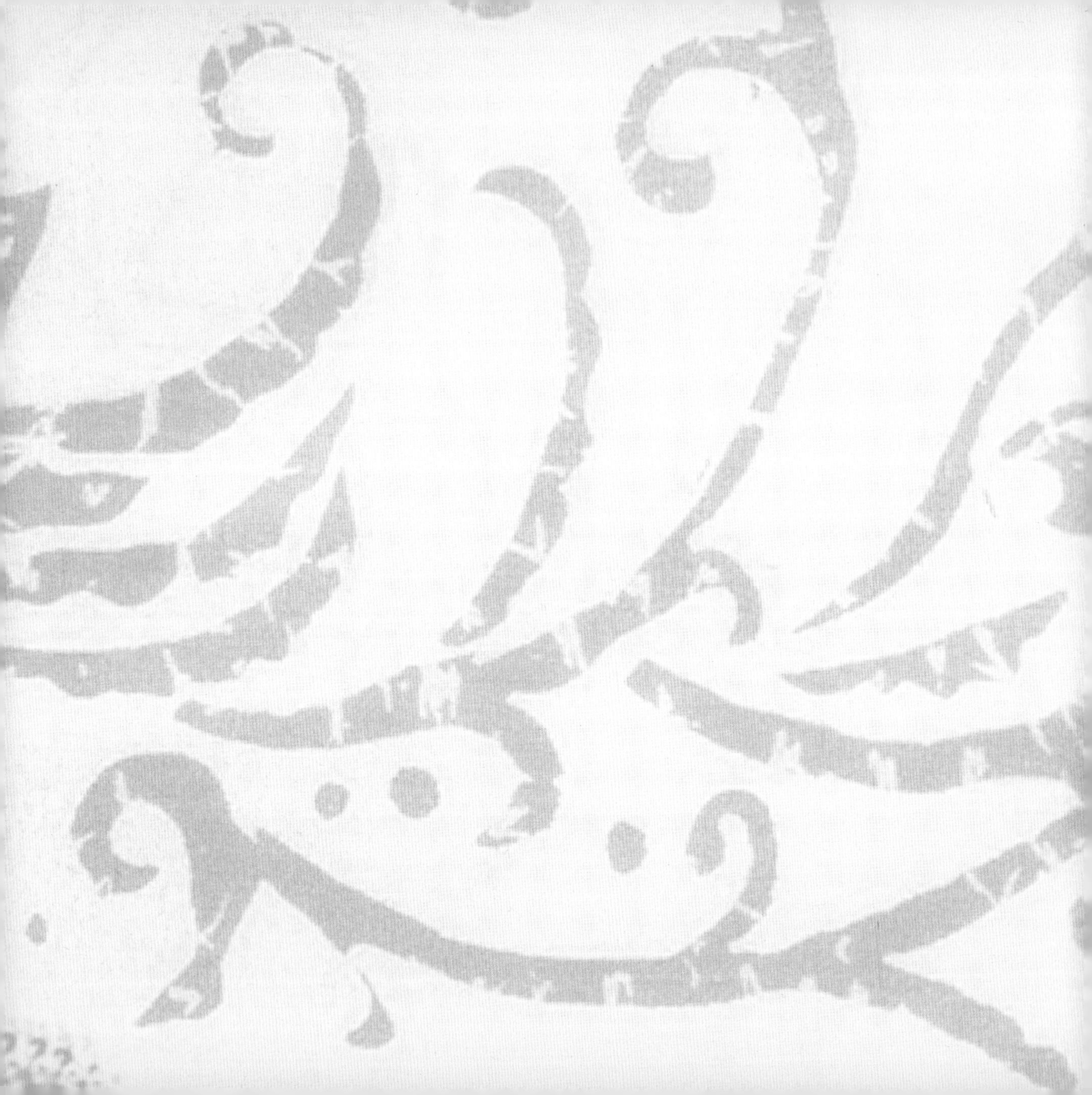

Big Thinker

Imagine yourself making a difference.
One that others could experience;
one that would be noticed in the world.

Now imagine this could be anything you wanted it to be.
That no matter how big or small,
it would be experienced by others.
It would be noticed in the world.

Does this interest you?
Does this inspire curiosity in you,
the you who wants to play big in the world?
There are four possible answers to this question.

- Yes
- No
- Yes, But
- Yes, AND...

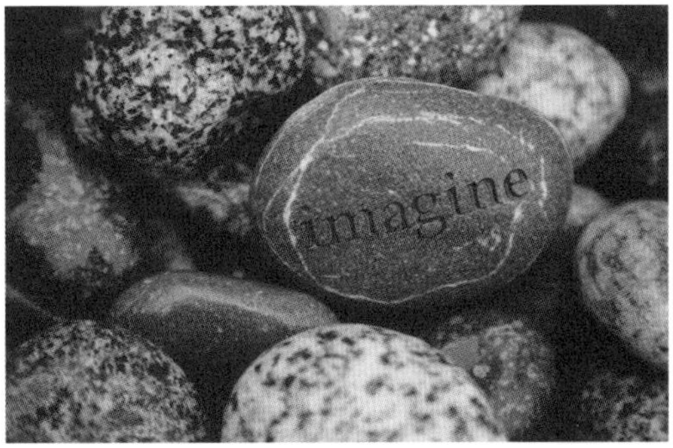
imagine

In the Spirit of Leadership | A Vision Into A Different Future

Courage

You hear a lot of talk these days about leadership and authenticity. A component of the coaching process for leaders is to help them stand in their truth, so that they can feel okay about what it is that they know to be true. I hear a lot from people that they can't be who they are, that they can't take their whole self to work. They can't show up and talk about their politics, their spiritual beliefs. They keep that completely hidden. And what I've seen over time is that people hold so much of themselves back that their spirit begins to die. If you are hiding part of yourself, you are not feeding part of yourself. People don't know who you really are, and they only respond to half of who you are, the half you are putting out there. Authenticity requires vulnerability… and that takes tremendous courage.

❧

Things To Think About

What part of your self do you not want to reveal?

❧

Courage

She arrives. Her stance is rigid, gripping a notepad to her chest. She smiles though her eyes are searching.

My listening is to her call to be here, to ask for help. Her story is filled with joy and disappointment, courage and fear.

Extraordinary people doing extraordinary things in the world of leadership. They want more. There is a knowing in them. To touch that is to see bigger, to move in grace, to make a difference in the world.

As she settles in, her body lets go, her voice softens. She tells me about the world of her career. She wants more.

People come to me for leadership coaching. To coach the leader who is them.

❧

5

Something More

I hear that there is a need
to do something that matters
that will
make a difference
to someone.
I hear that they are "spending" their time
doing
things that are less than meaningful.
I hear that the connections and love
in their lives are what make it all
worth doing...
and yet—a knowing
that there is more...
I hear they want to connect
with the natural world
and to breathe...they want to take long walks
and not be thinking
about their job, the laundry, etc.
I hear...
that they want to learn
presence...

&

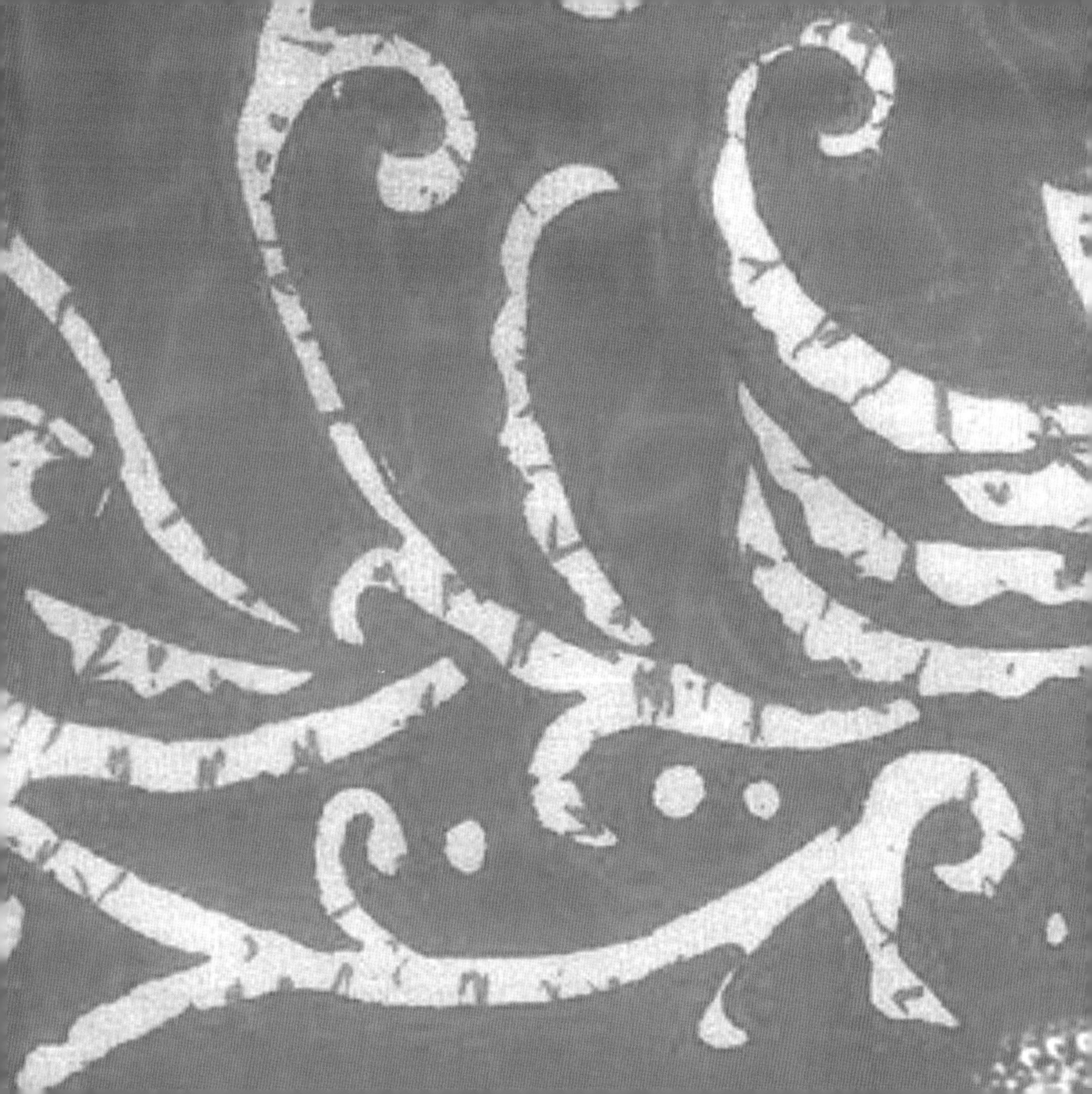

In the Spirit of Leadership | A Vision Into A Different Future

Being Leadership

Have you ever had the experience of attending a seminar, spending several days offsite and coming back with a great deal of knowledge? During the sessions you find yourself doing a lot of head nodding – these concepts make sense to you. "Good reminders," you think. "I must do more of this one."

For the first week, the noticed behavior improves, and then reality sets in, deadlines occur, a global partnership dissolves, stockholders get nervous. The board is watching closely. The last thing on your mind is being vigilant about a small behavior change in yourself – the key phrase being, "on your mind." In my years of consulting and coaching leaders, I noticed early on that knowledge around techniques and concepts created a framework for leadership behavior. And – often there was little to no foundation to support the framework.

We all do it – learn, apply, slip, revert, oh well.

This is where the body comes in. Embodied leadership. Being leadership. Different from being a leader. Being leadership occurs at our core, our essence, the unchanging constant of who we are. To touch this, one must quiet the being, let the distractions of the outer world fall away for a while. With that, clarity happens.

❧

Things To Think About

Where's the quiet in your life?

❧

The Place

The Place.
Ease and Grace.
Connecting.
Nurturing.
Deepening.
A welcome place.
My breath is long.
I slow my pace.
Tension has no being here.
Souls are touched.
Spirits are inspired.
It is safe to be me to connect deeply to see the world clearly
Rich conversations.
Real conversations.

A man is sitting quietly in the great room.
The outside flows in... through the enormous glass doors...nature is inside.

A woman joins him, the conversation gentle, mirroring the atmosphere. There is
no need for the requisite chatter politic. There is rhythm in the respect and genuine
interest each has for the other.

I know your value in the world. Tell me. There is an understanding between them.
There is a knowing – each is significant in and of the world. Each honors the other. The
conversation flows easily as others wander in, completely invited into the dialogue.

There are moments, many of them, that are enough. Without words. No discomfort.
Room for the silence. It is natural in its richness.

The man who was sitting quietly becomes the observer of the ease in the room. It is a
fortunate spirit that allows the dance.

Dancing alone is heady.

Dancing with others is exhilarating!

ॐ

Your body knows

So here I am, an hour early!
The morning is early
Skiing the fields of white
Floating at moments
Flying… mostly flying…
Face down, rolling over & over, sliding down
the steep slopes of white
The air dry and crisp
my feet unsure, excited
I am hanging on, looking down
Trust, trust he says
Lean forward, let your body be supported
Turn to the right, don't hold back
lean toward the downhill
side of the mountain – it is safe, it
gives you control
Try to resist it & you go faster, out of control
Holding back creates chaos. Your body knows.
Forget your brain. Your body knows –
it wants to move forward. Your body knows – it can
trust the open, vast world at your feet.
Your brain says get it right before you move
or the mountain will eat you up.
Your body knows. Trust. Trust. Your body knows.

&

Movement

The heart is movement—without effort.
It powers the body,
moves the fuel.
When I pay attention
it lets me feel it
in action.

The heart is moved—when connection happens,
when excitement happens,
when uncertainty becomes fear.
The heart is still—well, not really.
It only seems that way
when I am unconscious
when I am moving through the world
without intention
without purpose
without risk to connect,
to excite,
to experience uncertainty.

❧

Standing Still

There is no place in our culture for cocooning to happen along the career track. Cocooning is allowed during times of grief or recovery from illness. Even when we "take a sabbatical" which is viewed as more acceptable, it is not expected that we will stop doing, but will do something different.

Research has shown that when the butterfly is cocooning, it literally turns into soup. Even that soup is alive, there is energy, vibration, some sort of life force in it. This is what happens to us when we cocoon – even though it feels like mush, there's still something happening.

Things To Think About

What does cocooning look like for you?

What happens when you need to cocoon and
you don't let yourself, you can't or you won't stop?

৵

Cranky

Does it ever get better?
I want normal – whatever that is.
I want to want to move in the world.
Or maybe not.
Maybe I want to crawl under a rock.
This is not an option.
Enough standing still.
Enough freezing up.
But moving...moving is fun at first...then
tiring...
My friends say when will you do... fill in
the blank... – the retreat center; get more
clients; do that writing;
I am not living up to expectations.
Theirs. Mine. The universe.
Enough.

ॐ

Confidence

Confidence
is fleeting
Muscle is building
Informing my brain
with each moment
Where am I today?
Today is a good day –
Meaning I can count them
easily.
It seems that –
Why is it that –
going from neutral
to uninspired is
more consistent
than neutral to confident?

Well, that's better
than uninspired
to uninspired –
that used to
be the norm.
Neutral
is a relief
And actually
feels happy…
somewhat content –
Except when it
doesn't
and I think
about what I'm
not doing
And the
slow pace I am
keeping
And the
road ahead
seems so long –
To where,
I'm not sure.

æ

In the Spirit of Leadership | *A Vision Into A Different Future*

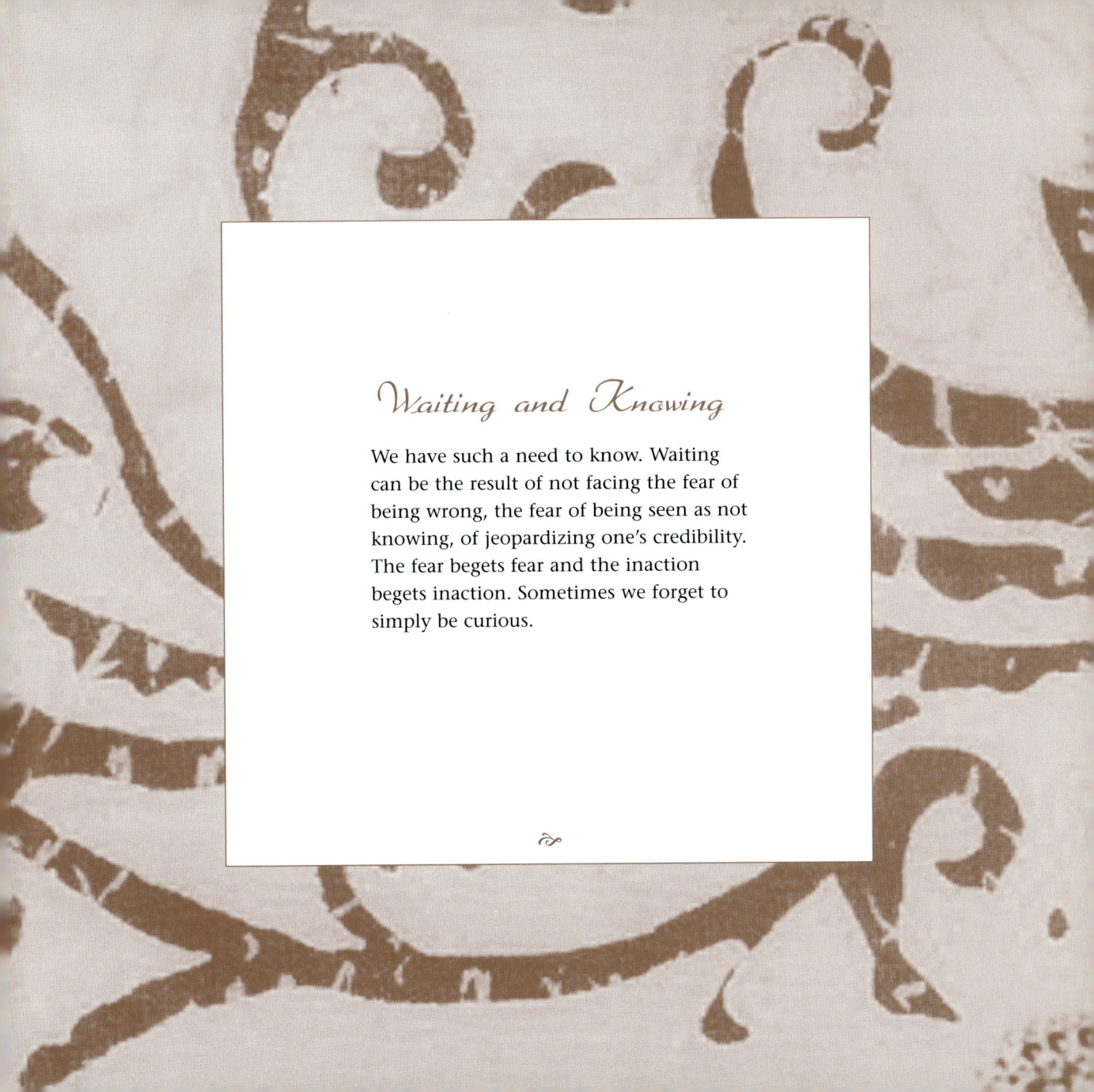

Waiting and Knowing

We have such a need to know. Waiting
can be the result of not facing the fear of
being wrong, the fear of being seen as not
knowing, of jeopardizing one's credibility.
The fear begets fear and the inaction
begets inaction. Sometimes we forget to
simply be curious.

&

Things To Think About

What's the worst thing that can happen if you are wrong
or seen as not knowing?

What would be the best case scenario if you were wrong?

Who can you talk to about the fear and the idea of taking action?

୶

Waiting

Waiting
A safe place.
A place of looking
from the inside out
of watching
others in action
myself still
The stillness is
at once quiet
and screaming…
!Are you in there?!
Do you have a
thought?
Of course, but
it's too early
to say
It may be wrong
not enough
or too much?
too real?

A requirement
to act, risk,
be visible,
ask for help
be a stand for
something
that others may
dismiss, then
I may believe
what if they're right
and I've been
waiting all this
time with the
wrong idea….

ॐ

One morning while I was at my desk, two large sea gulls perched on my window ledge and started tapping on the window for about 10 minutes! A delightful way to begin my day!

Sea Gulls

Surprise!
Hello....anybody there?
Can I come in?
Is there food in there?
Curious.
I'm finally curious.
I'm infinitely curious.

My adult says it's O.K.
My child says don't ask questions.
Ah – that means I must know the answers.

Already.
Without asking.
Without being curious.

Just know.
...How...?
How do we know...?
Anything?

Some say it's all there
For the taking.
For the knowing.

I know that.
I have been that.
I believe that.

I don't have anything to say.
I don't have anything to say.
Yes I do.
I'm curious.
What is knowing anyway?

⮞

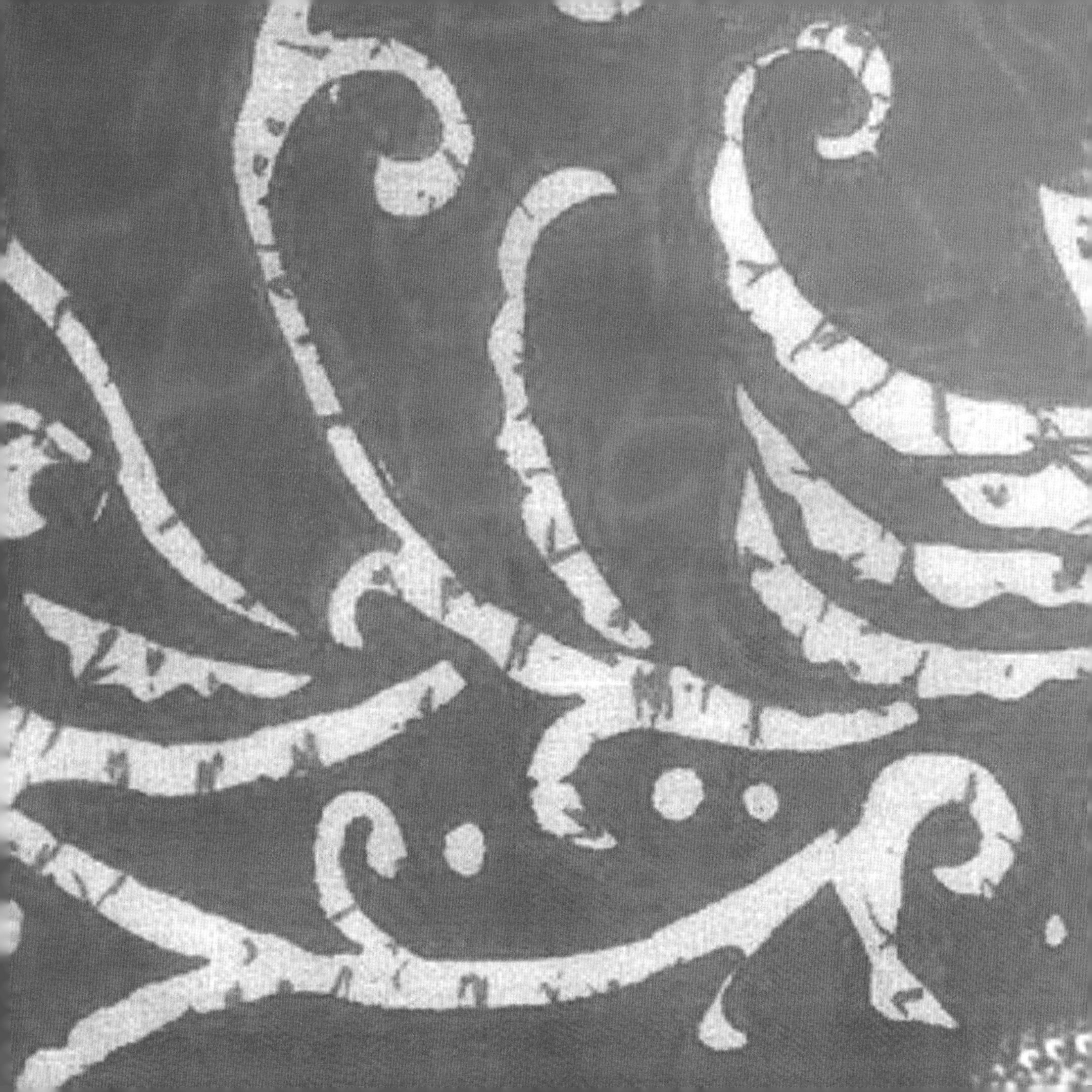

The Lonely Listener's Landscape

The Lonely Listener is a presence that lives inside of you. This is the one who believes that asking for help or sharing vulnerability is a sign of weakness. The one who believes it is necessary to have all the answers for others, be the rock, have the strong shoulders to hold everybody else up.

To do this is dismissing the self, discounting one's own needs. I see this in people of all roles, all backgrounds, all levels of responsibility. Ultimately this is about not feeding oneself to the point of not having enough to give back. Not having the energy to be that listener anymore.

☙

Things To Think About

How do I nourish myself?

How do I listen?

When am I lonely?

❧

The Lonely Listener's Landscape

Vast, open, able to accept so much, whatever comes. This canyon. Quiet except for the birds, the water, the boulder that says I can no longer hold on. I am leaving, letting go, moving on. Still strong. Still purposeful.

The lonely listener is a constant. Feels soft towards others. Strong and open. Their words, their love, their grief, their heart, their soul. Space to fill, still much much more.

The lonely listener is getting tired. When she speaks her loneliness, others leave. Can't hold it. Don't believe it. It must be passing. She will be fine. Doesn't need my help. "You have everything – why are you worrying? It will all work out."

Yes. It will all work out. What am I worrying about? Nothing significant.

&

I was listening

I was listening
I was holding my breath
"If someone else will say it,
I can just nod my head.
Then I can breathe."
Someone else is not saying it...
the it that wants to come out of me
The moment arrives it is time to speak
      while holding my breath...

Holding it in from the world
I can stay invisible

ɸ

There was a time when my energy around work shifted dramatically. I had always been a hard driver, a high achiever, daring anybody to say I couldn't do something because I would show them that I could do anything. Much later I would name that drive – that energy – the tyrant in me, even though from the outside, people might not have viewed it as tyrannical. Inside me, that's how powerful the energy was.

At some point my being, my energy, ran out of juice. The drive to prove myself day in and day out was no longer there. And without that drive I had no idea how to be, how to show up day in and day out. All I knew was that I was so tired.

One night in the midst of the exhaustion I had a dream. There were many elements to the dream, but in one particular part, I saw a lion devour a defenseless fox. I knew that stepping in to do something about it would only get me killed. In the dream I decided to put it in the category of 'well, that's what nature's all about', and left it alone. I didn't run, I just stood there and watched. The lion…was my tyrant. The fox…was me.

After that dream, I wrote a letter to the Tyrant. I could feel there was a shift.

Ask Yourself

What is chasing you?

Is it driving you or draining you?

How does your drive or exhaustion affect others?

～

Dear Tyrant,

You certainly showed your power and what you
are capable of. It was impressive.
I felt a respect for that power. Like I respect
the king of the jungle or the waves of the ocean.
It is when I do not respect that level of power
that I am in danger.
You seemed desperate to feed on that fox. Were
you starving?

I am wondering
I did not turn and run. I watched with
curiosity and a knowing that
it is best not to try to engage or for sure
not get in your way. Simply appear
to be no threat at all. Silent and
still.

But I did not turn and run. I stayed to face the
scene. Not easy to see, yet my
respectful curiosity kept me looking.

I am uncomfortable.
Thinking I should ask the question: is it
possible for us to talk? To be somehow
as partners? That feels too close. I feel I need
to go slow. To be sure. Yet I feel that
time is passing and it is important to
move on this.

32

Can I do this without you? Can I leave you
where you are & do this alone? That feels
safer. Then I am asking nothing of you
& I don't have to interact or
negotiate. I won't bother you. The truth
is I fear you. In a respectful way of course.
I fear you will win. Stop me from doing
what I need to do, want to do.
Stop me from the feeling of joy
& contentment & the experience of ease.
There is tension in you and always looking.
Not trusting.
I'm not sure what to do. I am
not sure I want to ask you to have
this conversation. I feel that you hold the
power. I will be devoured. Again. It is easier
safer to be silent and still.

છ

In the Spirit of Leadership | A Vision Into A Different Future

Falling Silent

There is an internal dialogue that exists in many of us. When we fall silent for a long time, afraid to speak what we believe, we begin to go numb so that we don't feel the pain of the silence. When that happens, to see things from the inside out, it's like standing and observing the world from inside your body without participating; stepping out of the game or off the game board for a time. You lose your place, and the internal dialogue is so strong and condescending.

❧

Things To Think About

Who is talking in your internal dialogue?

If you were numb, how would you know?

What are the conversations you are not having?

*When I see my clients having shut down in their roles at work,
in their roles in their family, in their life...this is where the
numbing begins. They begin to believe that they have no voice, no
power to change the status quo especially if it appears to be going
against the grain. People fall silent in an effort to survive. The
problem is survival doesn't begin with silence; it begins with
clarity in yourself. Then you can make the move that matters.*

᷂

Numb

Numb.
Numbness.
One letter from dumb.
Dumbness.
Dumb defined as not able to speak.
Silenced vocal cords
Silenced in the world
Seeing.
Seeing with desire.
Seeing with fear
Seeing with "I want to…I can't."
It won't happen
I'm not smart enough.
No one will believe me
"How nice dear.
We used to believe you,
But now it's
Different.
You've been dumb too long.
You can't even
Speak
What you see now."
Now.
It's now
That matters.
Now…
That is the truth
Of the future.

Confused.
"What? I don't understand. I want…"
"Of course you do dear.
But
Dumb people
Aren't taken seriously."
So you must be numb
To the world
To survive.
It's easier,
Less pain.
Safer.
No one
will call you
dumb.
Just silenced.
Nothing
Of substance.
Disappear.
Remember
Your invisible self…

Ah, but I burned my invisible self!
In the fire.
Gone.
Only ashes now.
Out of the ashes, the phoenix
Rises.
Powerful enough
To speak
Without speaking
Knowing. Seeing. Respected.
I am that now
Silence is the practice of seeing, knowing what I know.
Giving voice to the silence. Powerful.
Power.
Full.
Full.
Spilling out / over / creating new shapes.
Feeling / felt / found.
Feeling it.
Felt by others.
Found the voice.
Power.
Full.

ॐ

This is an invitation into self-acceptance, self-knowing, the comfort of being inside the stillness. Being gentle with oneself.

Love Notes to Myself

Tired.
The body.
The muscles
The movement
Slow
Now motionless.
Still.
Feel the stillness.
Awaken
Inside the stillness.
There is knowing
In stillness.
Listen.
It is speaking
Softly
Easily.
Whispering
Love notes in the stillness
To myself.
I never noticed…
Love notes to myself.

୭

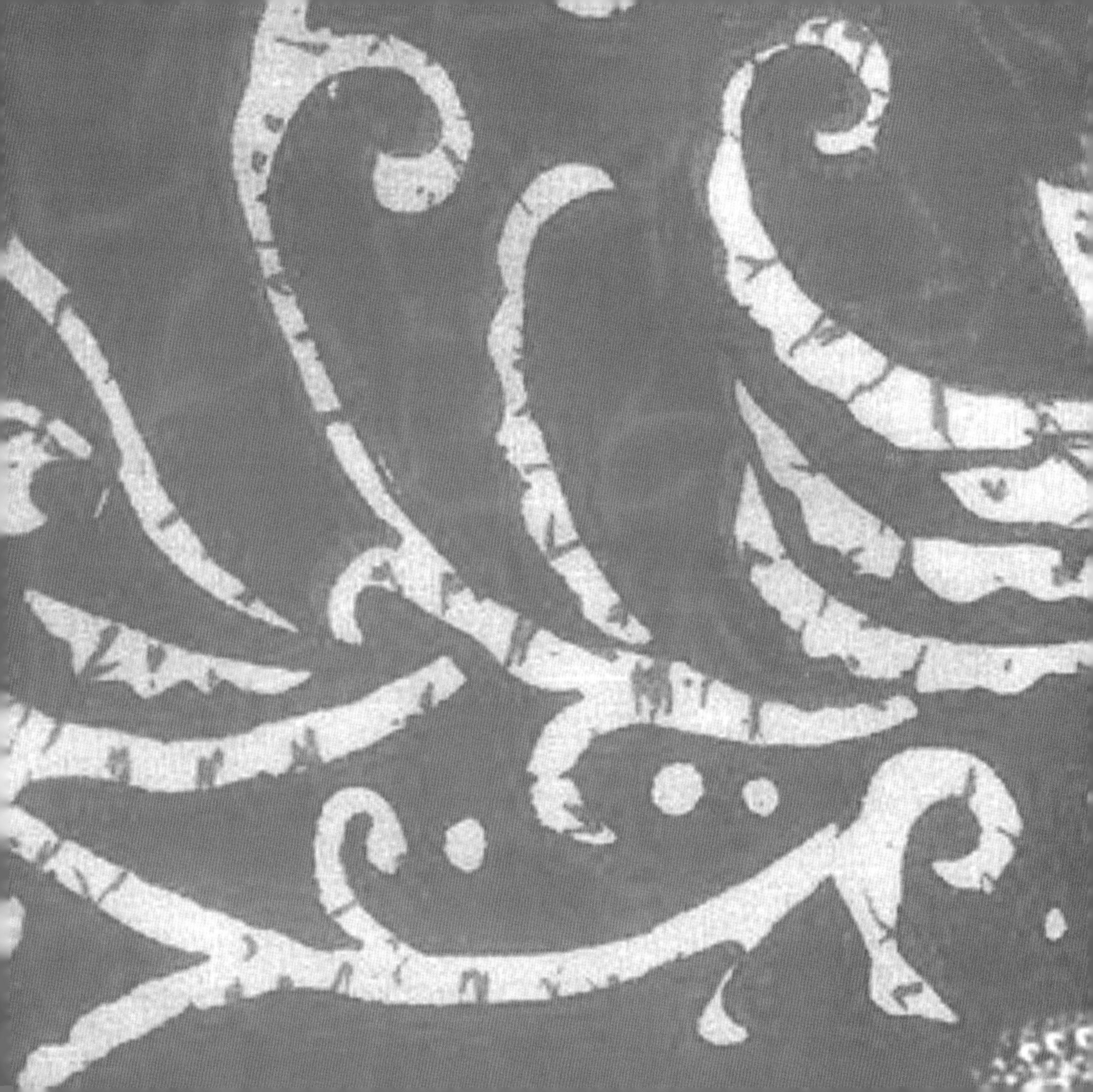

In the Spirit of Leadership | *A Vision Into A Different Future*

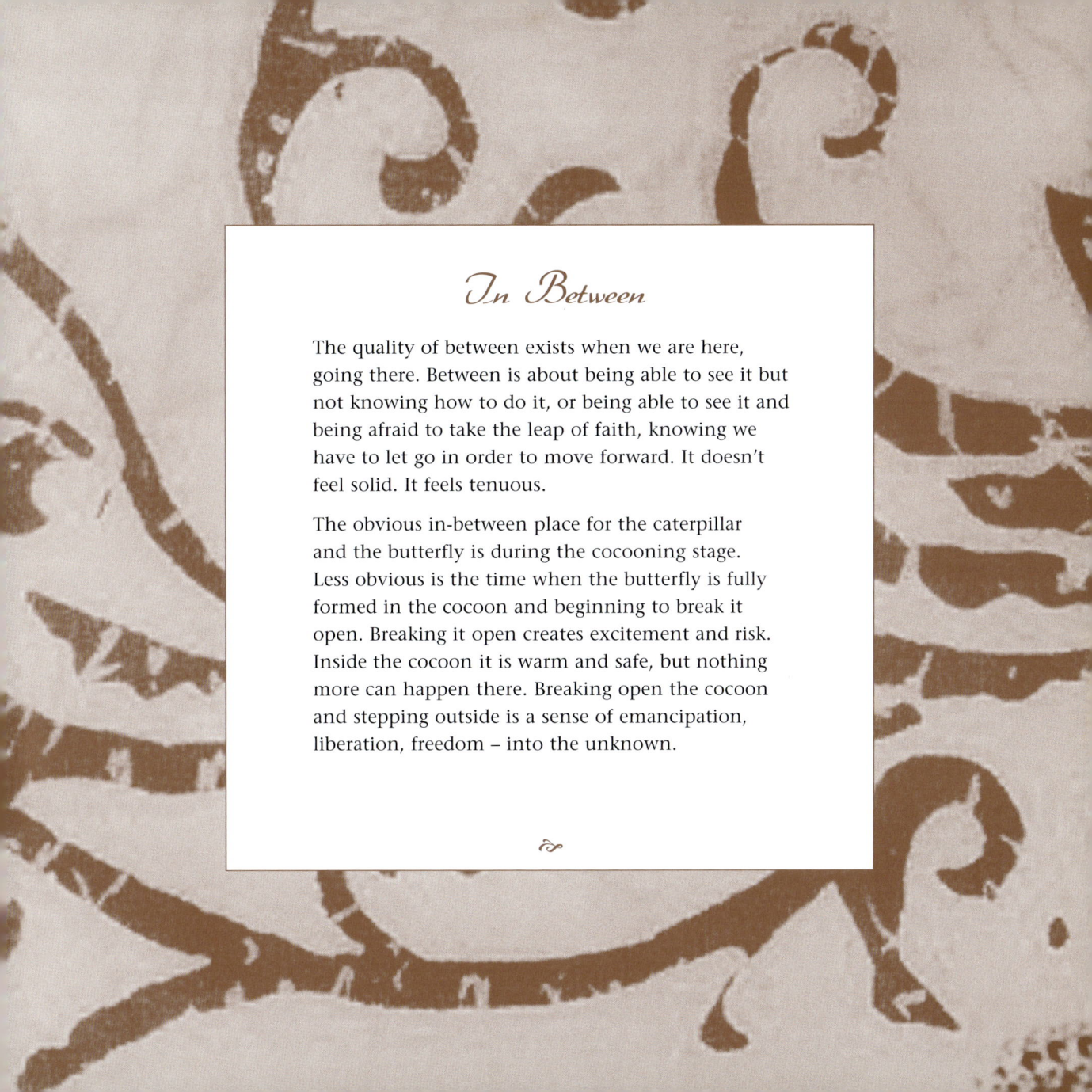

In Between

The quality of between exists when we are here, going there. Between is about being able to see it but not knowing how to do it, or being able to see it and being afraid to take the leap of faith, knowing we have to let go in order to move forward. It doesn't feel solid. It feels tenuous.

The obvious in-between place for the caterpillar and the butterfly is during the cocooning stage. Less obvious is the time when the butterfly is fully formed in the cocoon and beginning to break it open. Breaking it open creates excitement and risk. Inside the cocoon it is warm and safe, but nothing more can happen there. Breaking open the cocoon and stepping outside is a sense of emancipation, liberation, freedom – into the unknown.

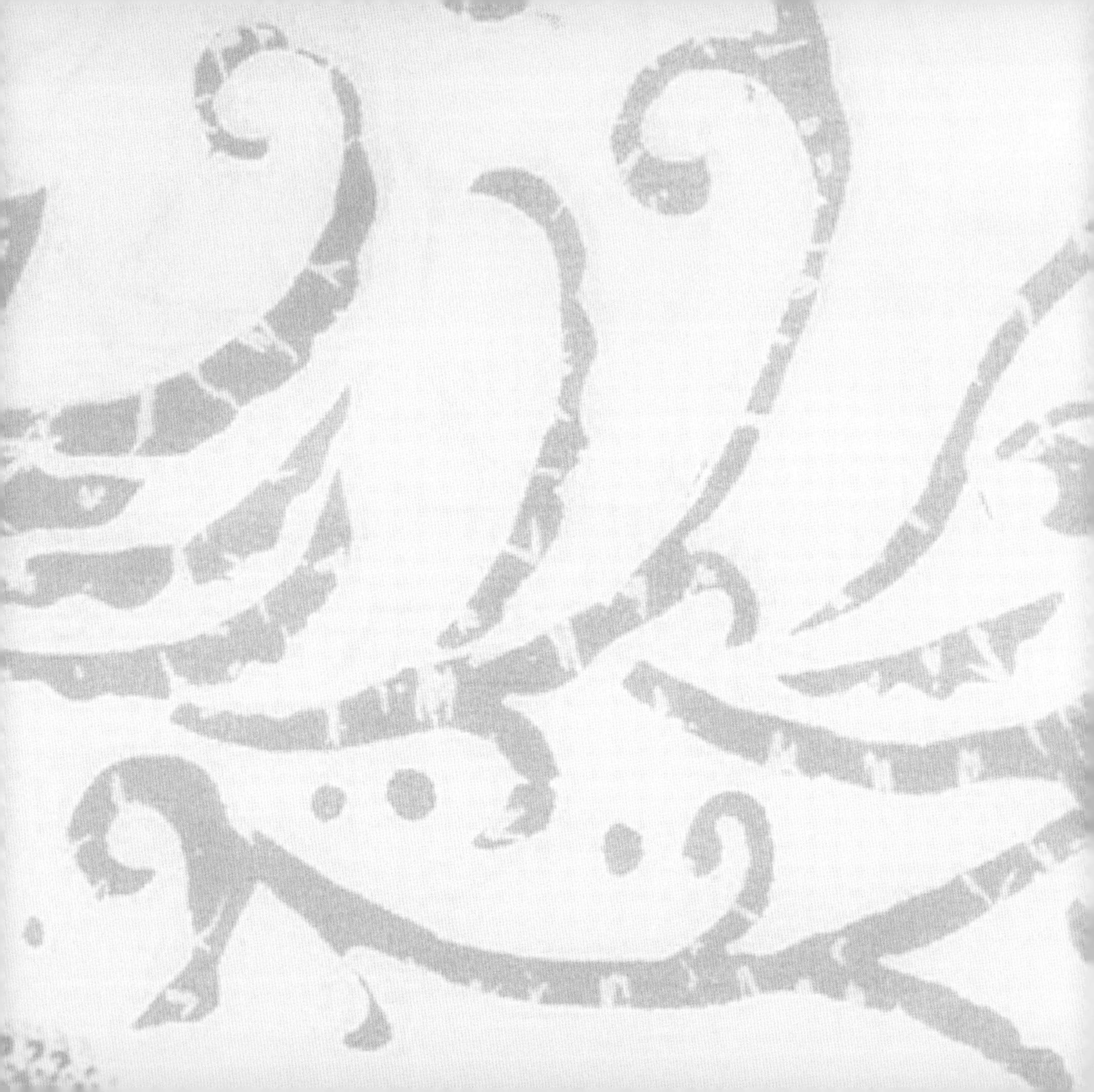

The time in between

The time in between
Has many in betweens...
The chasm seems wide
from here to there
Then a knowing...
many small chasms
to cross before
reaching the other side...
where a new
in between
begins...

❧

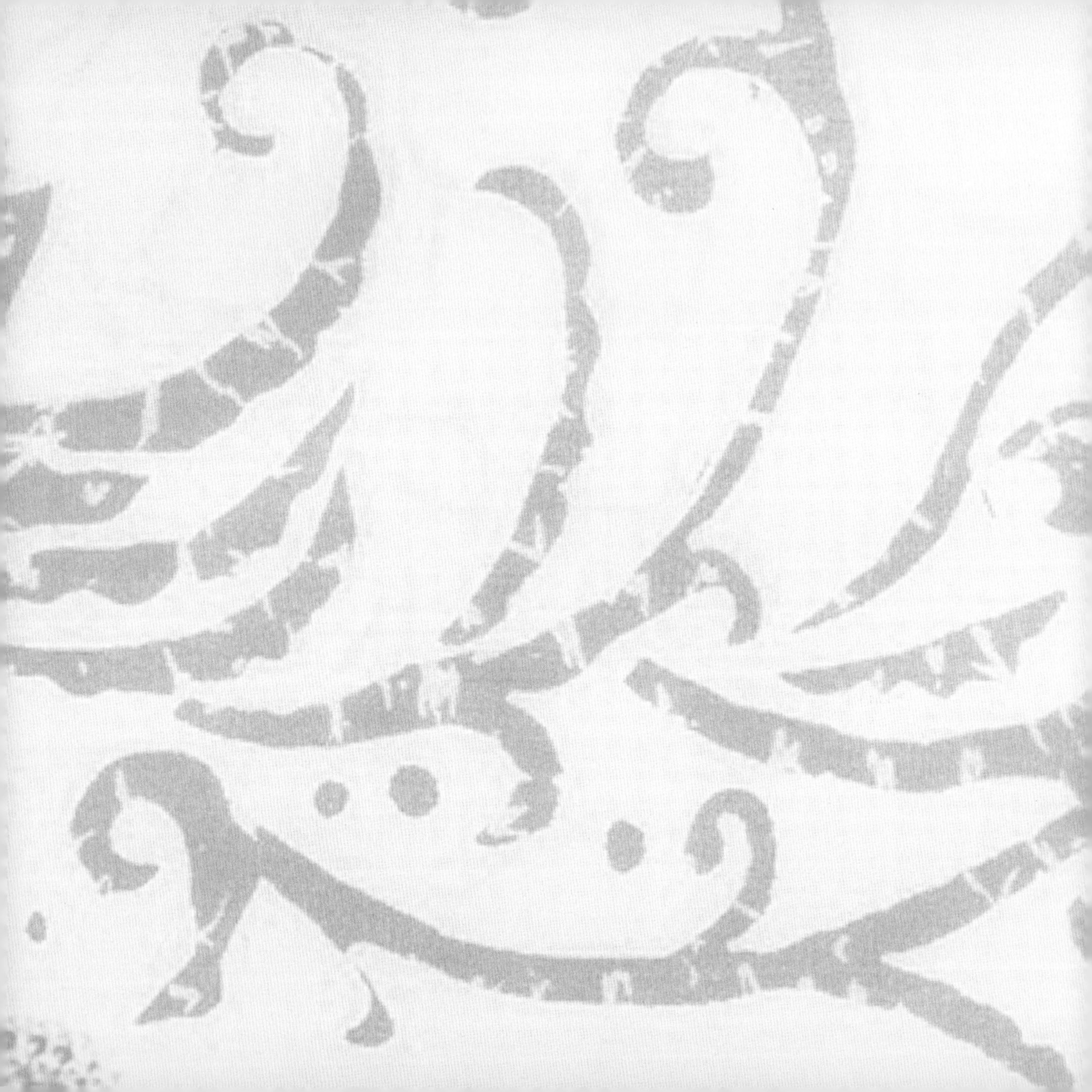

The Trapeze 1

The next step
From here to there
The in between
The abyss
The blackness
The black hole

What if... I don't know...
I don't know what if...
What would I do?

What if it doesn't work?
What if it does?

Then I better do it well
Then I'm committed
Then things change

Letting go
To grab on
The trapeze
There is a net,
Isn't there?
It's hard to land on your feet
On a net
You flounder and falter
And roll and bounce

And unless you know how
You even need help with that –

With getting out of the net
Back on your feet
Back on solid ground.   ✺

The Trapeze 1   The Trapeze 1a

The next step	Is right in front of me.
From here to there	Are lots of questions.
The in between	Can be exciting.
The abyss	Opens up wide.
The blackness	Allows for anything to be painted on it
The black hole	Will be safe, but stopping…
What if… I don't know…	I will ask.
I don't know what if…	Yes I do. I will ask.
What would I do?	I will ask.
What if it doesn't work?	I will ask a different question
What if it does?	I will be excited
Then I better do it well	Okay
Then I'm committed	That's right
Then things change	Yup
Letting go	Is scary
To grab on	Is courageous
The trapeze	Can hold me
There is a net,	
Isn't there?	Yup
It's hard to land on your feet	
On a net	Yup
You flounder and falter	
And roll and bounce	That could be fun
And unless you know how	
You even need help with that –	So there may be a way to do it
	So it works for me
	So I'll ask about that
With getting out of the net	
Back on your feet	To get me back – Back on my feet,
Back on solid ground.	Back on solid ground.

48

The Trapeze 2

The Trapeze
Can hold me.
It is the space in between –
How odd.
Hold tight!
Swing big!
Let go!
Grab on!
Hold tight.
So fast.
So much ease
Ease.
Grace.
Ahhh…

❧

In Between

There it is again.

There it is again.
That in between.
That place of uncertainty
That place where everything
is possible
and nothing
feels right.

The in between shows up all around me
In this writing I am in between.
The words are in between.
I am so good at seeing
what's in between –
for others...
hearing the unspoken,
in between the words –
for others...
I listen.
I listen.
The lonely listener is
alive and well...in me.
How do I put her to work *for* me?
What are the words
from the place
in between
that she will hear?

Oh.
She does hear.
I just don't know it
because
I'm in that place
of uncertainty.
That place where everything
is possible...
and nothing
feels right.

꙰

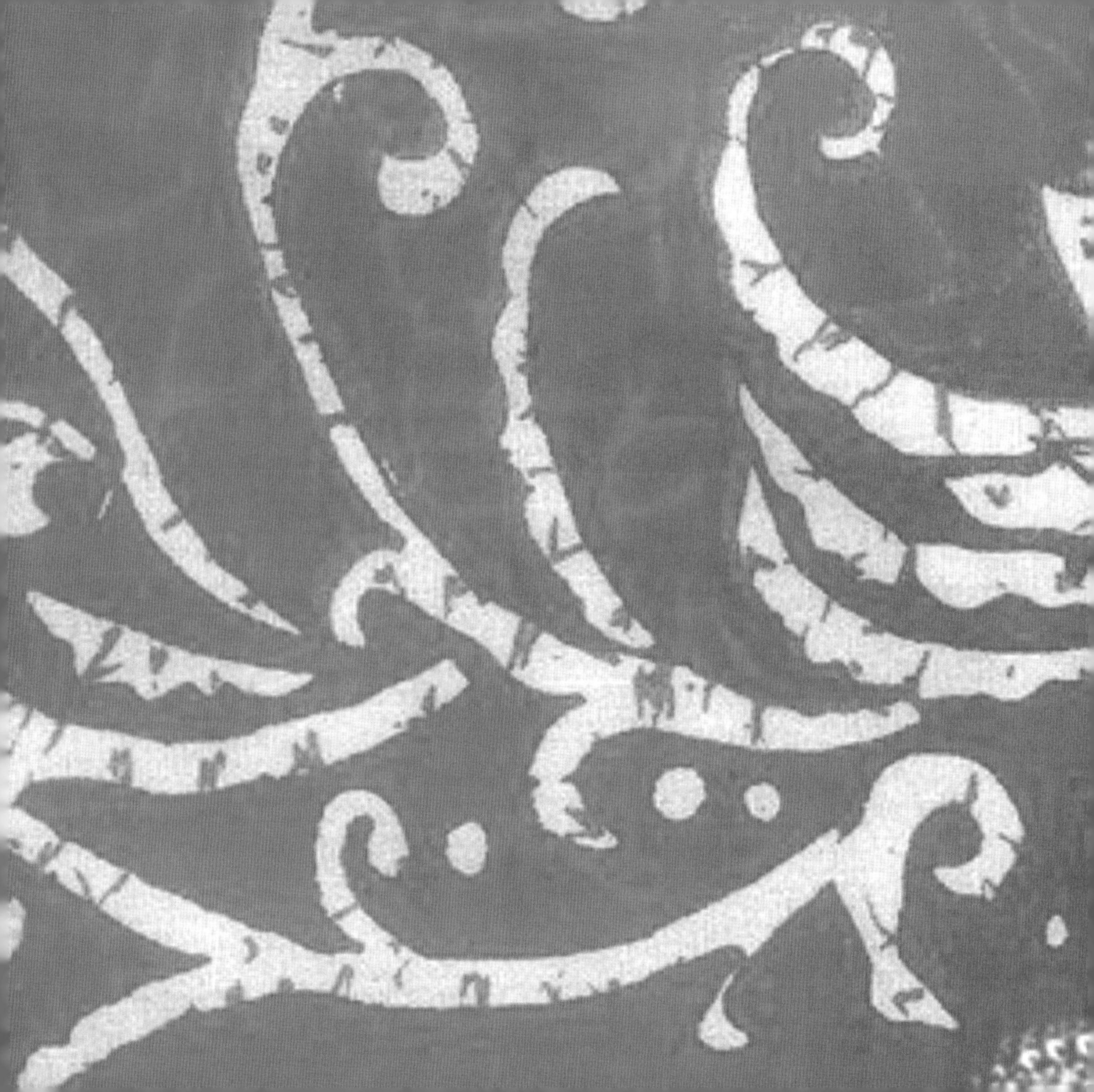

In the Spirit of Leadership | *A Vision Into A Different Future*

Being Seen

Wilderness solo is a cocooning of sort. There I experience slowing down enough to actually hear my thoughts (some helpful, others not!) I have responsibility only to myself (inner nature) and to the land and animals (outer nature). Life becomes so simple.

When I share with my clients that I am going off into the wilderness to do a solo, they say "why?" I say, "so that I can be here and show up with clarity, for you, for all my clients. So 'my own stuff' doesn't blur my vision when I look at you. So I can be fully present to do this work with you." I am fascinated with the idea that it is easier to see and be seen after you haven't been for a while.

Summer 2005 I did a 28-day solo in Crestone, Colorado. I had done many wilderness solos in the past, none as long as this. There were moments when I made choices about feeling fearful and taking action in the face of it. There were moments when I froze in terror, certain that I heard a bear, only to see a squirrel dashing between trees. Keeping a sense of humor and not taking oneself too seriously is a potential side effect in this work. Truly practice for my life!

On solo, lots of things can happen. Everything has meaning. Some of the experiences are big and obvious, and some are subtle, simple, small. The point is, every moment matters.

Being Overly Dramatic

Oh, please.
Yes. O.K. so the bear came to visit.
The marines swept the beach
The rattlesnake issued its warning
The wind pummeled the tent…
…all through the night…

But, please. Really.
It is nothing compared to what others
in the world
experience
day after day.

You have love.
You have partnership.
You have family.
You have,
you have,
you have.
So stop complaining and
stop the drama.

88

The fire –
Well, the fire was different.
And could have been worse.
"Can you walk down the mountain,
or are you too agitated?" asked
the rescue squad leader.
Even he thought I was
being overly dramatic.
Well. No. Actually he was
trying to discern the fastest
way to get me down the mountain.

People want to know.
So I tell them.
Then they don't want to know.
And I wish I hadn't.
So I answer their questions
one at a time.
I try to move the conversation
along – away from the fire.
They keep asking. I answer.
They want to know.
Then… they don't.
The story is dramatic. Intense.

They want to know,
then they don't.

"Oh my God.
You were on fire?!?
I can't imagine anything
anything
worse
to happen to a person.
That's horrible."

I think, well, yes.
It was horrible
but I lived through
it
I am here now
This does not define me.
Do not think of me
as that woman who
was burned in a fire.
Like damaged goods.

Exhausted.
This is too much.
Too much to hold.
Too much to feel.
Too much to think about.
Too much.
Too much.
Too much.

&

In the fire, I experienced extensive second degree burns. My healing happened fast. I had regular check ups at the burn unit, and while in the waiting room, would encounter family and friends of others who had suffered serious burns. Their suffering put my experience in perspective. This poem was written in the waiting room approximately six months after my original burn, during one of those visits.

The Waiting Room

Sitting.
Waiting & wondering
Images thoughts stories
Grateful
Compassion for others –
so much worse than me
at the beginning of their journey
Can I tell them, it gets better
You must have hope, believe in
yourself
Do not listen to the information
that says you will not be
completely normal
create your own reality
create my own reality – it is
my truth.
when people ask How is it doing?
Say, It is healing so well.

When they say How are you doing?
Say I am well. I am healing
so fast.
Image the healing. See the skin,
the protector of the body, growing smoothly
and quickly. It is responding. It is
healing. You are healing. I am healing.
We are healed.

࿇

Being Seen

Being Seen
    Watched
    Noticed
What happens when I catch them watching me?
I look away.
I feel self-conscious.
I notice my flaws.
I get embarrassed.
I watch myself
to know what they are watching.
Performance anxiety…
Need to look really good
better than normal
Feels impossible
Feels unreal
Feels
Feels
Feels
Until it's over.

∽

Sleep... or Not

I practice stretching, qi gong, tai chi and sometimes sitting in meditation (I like to choose from the menu.) I notice that when I have a bout of insomnia, I have not been doing any of my practices. Then it becomes a downward spiral because I feel too tired to do them.

The practice of presence is important here – when people have insomnia, they're not thinking about this moment. They're thinking about tomorrow, or what was done, or what has to be done. And often, the body hasn't been used, in exercise or any movement practice.

Sleep builds resilience, emotional and physical. Without it the self-talk and brain chatter can become saboteurs. Even when things are great, sometimes there's a snag. Having your self-talk as your ally has advantages. If you are well rested, it may only be a blip on the screen. Without quality sleep... well, you get the picture.

☙

Things To Think About

What has your self talk been like lately?

What can you do to enhance your
sense of well being?

⁊

Insomnia

We wait & see &
only see when we're
done waiting...

Last night I lay awake
waiting to go to sleep
waiting to stop thinking
waiting to feel myself drifting

seeing if I could close my
eyes & make myself go to sleep
except I can't see when
I close my eyes

And I wasn't done waiting...

&

Sleep

Sleep
Not Sleeping
The night goes on & on
The moments of sleep
are not sleep
I am skimming the
surface of reality
in and out of
consciousness
my mind is confused
Am I awake?
Why can't I go to sleep?
Slip away from
the reality of
responsibility
into the relief of
no expectations
no pressure to
act, to do, to be
any particular
way
that others
want
that I am
afraid of
that I fear is at last the only
way to go; It is
no longer acceptable to wait...even for me.

&

My mind is awake

My mind is awake
but not useful
My body craves the
satisfaction of slumber
of drifting into the arms
of the night

My mind is awake
and says "that would be
nice, go ahead"

An hour later my mind
is still saying, "that
would be nice, go ahead.
Go to sleep."

Another hour later
my mind is awake
and not useful.

The body has given up
the desire to sleep
I move from the bed
My mind says, get up
then maybe I'll get
tired enough to go
to sleep

An hour later my mind
is awake & not useful
and has stopped fighting
my body's desire
for sleep
Back in bed, snuggled in
Ahh…

An hour later my mind is awake but not useful.

෴

My mind is awake

My mind is awake
but not useful
My body craves the
satisfaction of slumber
of drifting into the arms
of the night

My mind is awake
and says "that would be
nice, go ahead"

An hour later my mind
is still saying, "that
would be nice, go ahead.
Go to sleep."

Another hour later
my mind is awake
and not useful.

The body has given up
    the desire to sleep
    I move from the bed
My mind says, get up
then maybe I'll get
tired enough to go
to sleep

An hour later my mind
    is awake & not useful
    and has stopped fighting
    my body's desire
    for sleep
    Back in bed, snuggled in
    Ahh…

An hour later my mind is awake but not useful.

√

It's Our Nature

No matter how many times I've packed for
solo, no matter how many Sacred Passages
I've gone on, the packing process doesn't
change for me. It's similar to preparing for a
big presentation, or preparing a big offer or
proposal. Everything needs to be just right.
Right gear, right stuff, right weight, right
just in case…

Things To Think About

How do you carry the weight of being a leader?

Is it well-balanced on your shoulders, in your body?

❧

Backpack

This is the part I hate.
The planning
The packing
The deciding
– my deciding
– his deciding
not always the same...
The imagining the cold dark nights
The animals. Mostly they see me
I don't see them
The conscious fear that I carry is my backpack
Maybe that's the problem...
Don't pack the fear
Leave it behind
It adds weight to the pack
Makes the hike in more challenging
Takes up space for...
for...
nothingness
being
for seeing
for clarity
for...
just takes up space.

Becoming

"Treat your body well,
your soul is taken care of..."
A new way of thinking –
soul, spirit, other than body...
The bent of much attempt or
study of spiritual development.
Except soma
In this we are "becoming..."
We are not separate pieces
struggling to be one;
we are one piece...
becoming...
The white sands of Baja
receive me as one
I choose or not to believe
that my work is to
connect and align mind
body spirit
The white sands of Baja smile
upon me as the sea
gently laps the shore
If I get too far out
the ocean for sure
has its way with me –
all of me... becoming....

෨

The water moves

The water moves – power and nurturance are one.
Inside it I float, buoyed and tossed and held
It's like life
Healthy respect is in order
love for what it is
its beauty
its touch
its requirement for life on this planet
The water moves – power & nurturance are one.
I struggle to hold both at once
which is more important – power or nurturance
which do I trust – power or nurturance
I want to let go
I want to step into the gentleness of
the waves spilling across the
wet sand
The water moves – power & nurturance are one
join me it says. I will be your partner.
You can dance with me.
You must be
strong: Powerful and nurturing.
We must be
partners. And I will respect you.
The water moves with me.
Our power
& nurturance
are
one.

☙

This Place

Wherever I am in the world – other than in my daily life –
the only responsibility
I have
is to myself
and to this place.
the self who is not
judged
the self who is not
concerned with the
pleasing of others
the self who simply is.
This place does not
judge
it embraces me
and forgives me
and teaches me
This place invites me
my curiosity
my wonder
my not knowing.
This place is big enough
to hold me and all of my
self doubt until there is no more
Until there is just me.
And this place.
Wherever I am in the world
the only real responsibility
I have
is to me
and to this place...
because I am
this place.

෨

Connecting with one's nature

Open space. Big sky. Canyons that are endless. There I can breathe. I feel everything. I am alone with my fear, with my joy, with my self.
Out there, I understand the insignificance of me…
And the significance of us, the humans inhabiting the earth. We are at once reckless and loving with the mother.
When I am there, I am vigilant with my care. I feel honored to be there.
There. To be there. To be.
I don't experience "there" during day to day living.
I see and appreciate,
but the "there" feeling is quiet.
I lose the nature within me.
In solo, I connect with my true nature.
No judgment – well, at least not so much after day 2…
I bring with me the experience of daily life, interactions, dilemmas. There I see them differently. I go deep. I cry I laugh I hold on I let go. I let go. I sleep. I breathe. I see. I see. I practice. I see – differently. Color, depth, beauty. It is all around me. Color, depth, beauty. I am this as I am of the mother. She says, "You reflect me. I will be as you. Be good to me, be good to you. Be reverent with yourself, be reverent with me."
And so it is.

ॐ

The year I went back to the land to do the longer solo, our group gathered for an evening meal. We were joined by Peter who is a member of the rescue squad and teaches the volunteer fire fighters. We talked about fire and my experience the year before. I told him that as I walked around the circle of the fire to figure out what to do, the flame was following me. I would go in one direction, and it would move with me. Peter says fire is alive; it's an energy force. It showed up for me because I was not touching the fire in my life, in my nature.

Ask Yourself

Where is the fire in your life?

❧

74

Fire is chasing me

Fire is chasing me.
It follows my footsteps
Dances on my breath
Fire is chasing me
It wants to know
where is the flame
where is the desire
for life
for living
for burning
The flame is alive
then it's not
How powerful it is
but we must control it.
    It may become
    too big
    too bright
    too magnificent
    too...uncontrollable.
Fire is chasing me...
The flame is alive in me.
Fire has found me...
Fire
is
me.

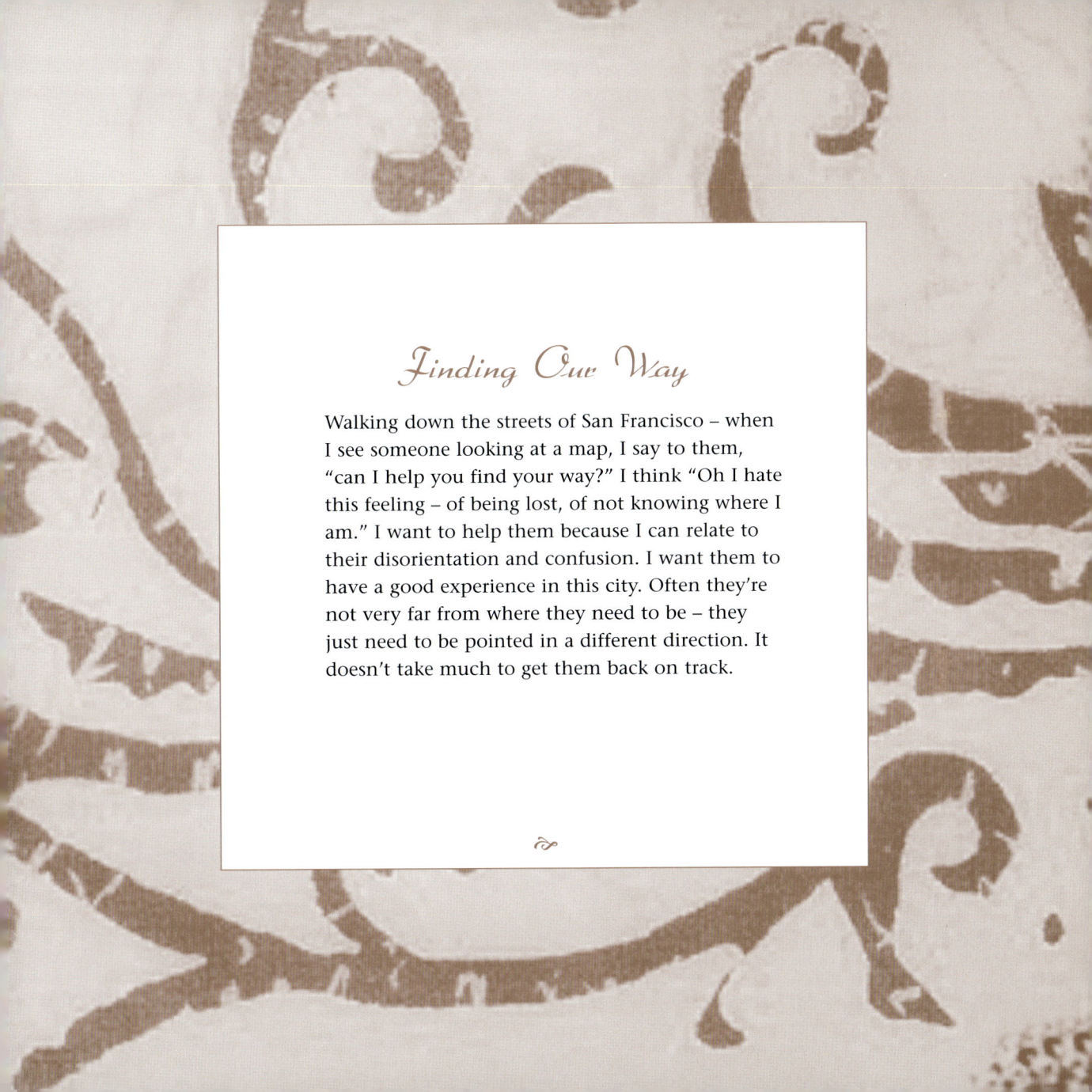

Finding Our Way

Walking down the streets of San Francisco – when I see someone looking at a map, I say to them, "can I help you find your way?" I think "Oh I hate this feeling – of being lost, of not knowing where I am." I want to help them because I can relate to their disorientation and confusion. I want them to have a good experience in this city. Often they're not very far from where they need to be – they just need to be pointed in a different direction. It doesn't take much to get them back on track.

☙

Things To Think About

When have you wished for help in finding
your way but felt it was not okay to ask?

To whom do you give permission to help
nudge you in a different direction?

Out There

out there

it is safe to be curious

we wander

we are welcomed

people offer their generosity

out there

we forget our day to day distractions –

our focus on self

we look and look and look

and experience a new way of being in this world

where we are not known

where there are no obligations

where time has little relevance

where all things seem possible…

out there…

It's how to bring out there in here that is the work…

❧

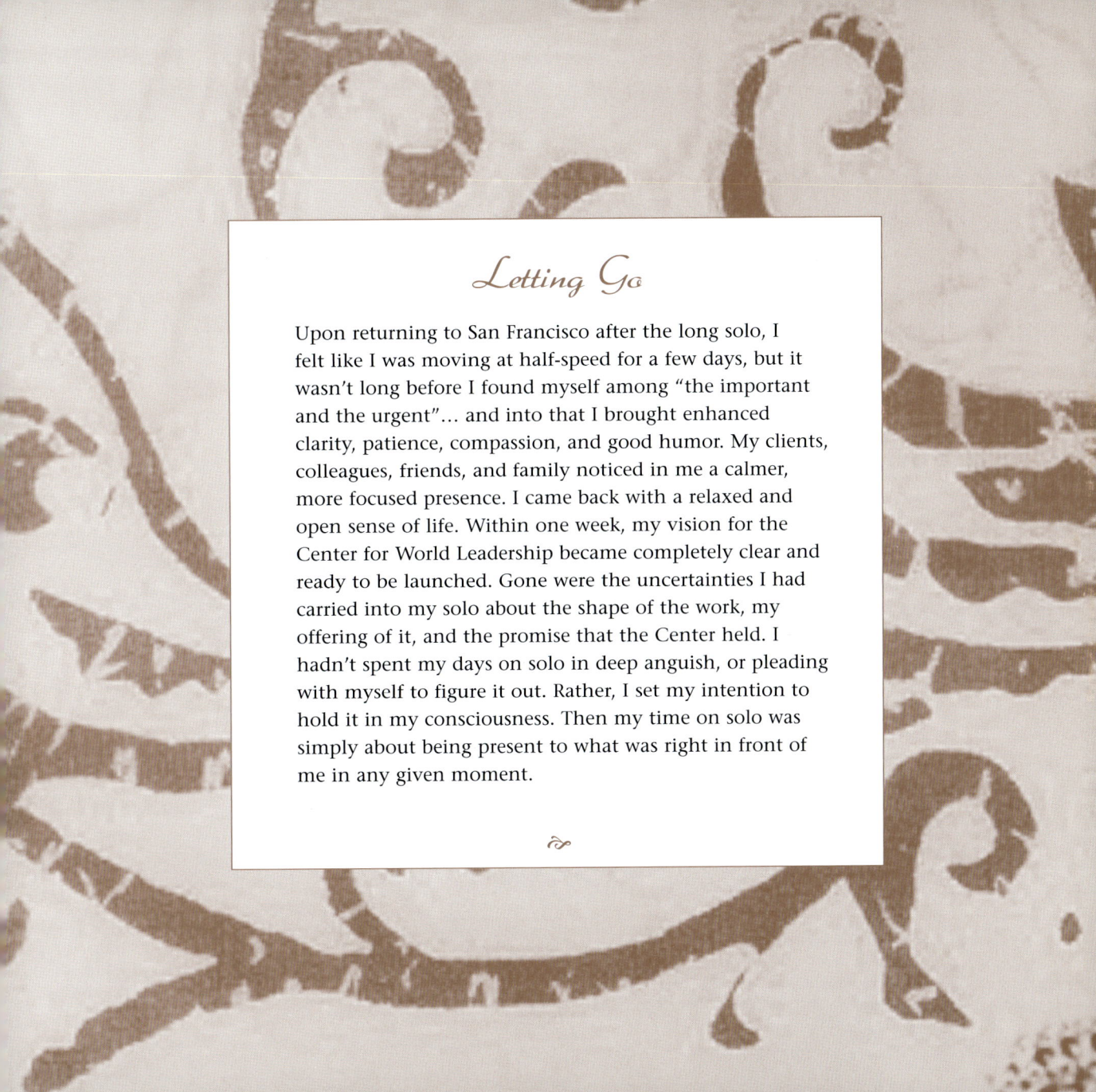

Letting Go

Upon returning to San Francisco after the long solo, I felt like I was moving at half-speed for a few days, but it wasn't long before I found myself among "the important and the urgent"... and into that I brought enhanced clarity, patience, compassion, and good humor. My clients, colleagues, friends, and family noticed in me a calmer, more focused presence. I came back with a relaxed and open sense of life. Within one week, my vision for the Center for World Leadership became completely clear and ready to be launched. Gone were the uncertainties I had carried into my solo about the shape of the work, my offering of it, and the promise that the Center held. I hadn't spent my days on solo in deep anguish, or pleading with myself to figure it out. Rather, I set my intention to hold it in my consciousness. Then my time on solo was simply about being present to what was right in front of me in any given moment.

⊱

Things To Think About

Take a break from your story.

See what emerges when you walk away. If you
are living in the story of "I don't know", until
you step out of the story, you won't know.

⁊

Moving forward

Moving forward by pulling back
Leaning in
Breathing
Lean In
Inhale
Pull Back
exhale
Lean In
Launch
Anticipate
Get Ready
Pull Back
exhale life into the effort
glide forward
Keep moving
If you keep moving
you'll keep moving...
You'll move faster with help.

❧

Stepping Out

Before you take a step
You must first know where that step will take you.

Before you take a step
You must know all the questions to ask.

What if...
You take a step...you courageously step out into the darkness
with no clear view...

What if...
You take a step...you wait for the questions to become
along the way...

What if...
You take a step...and you are not taken seriously
because you aren't giving others a structure
to contain your idea, your dream, your not knowing...

Before you take a step
You must remember
to step into the darkness with courage and wonder
to let the questions become—the ones even you cannot yet see
to let the dream take shape as you move...
it may be much bigger than
the container that others are comfortable with...

You must remember...
then...
you take a step.

ॐ

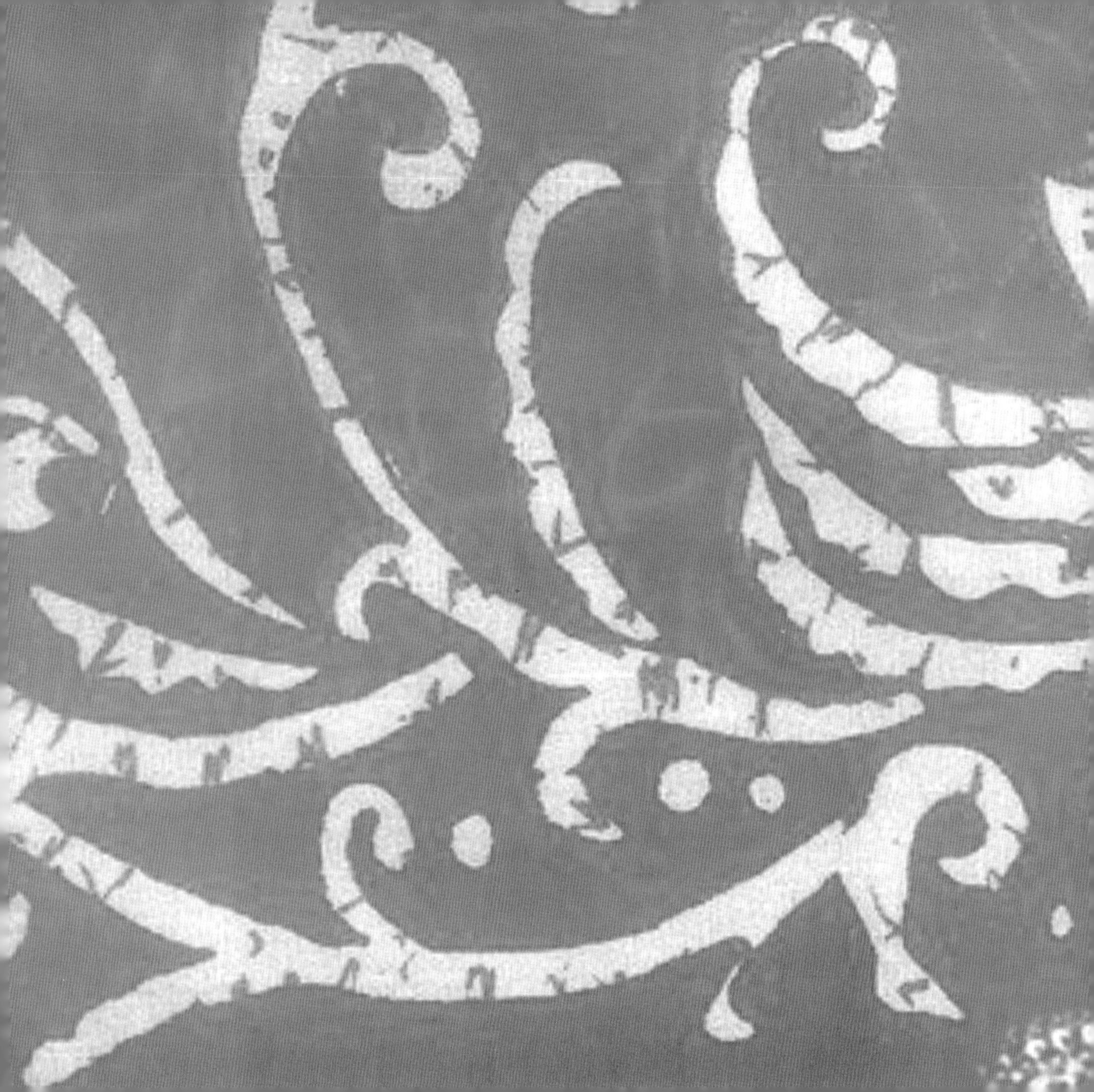

What Is

We often focus on what isn't rather than what is. We regret what was, we fear what could be, and we ignore what is.

Pay attention, feel your body. Practice awareness of each moment. Powerful leaders and coaches live here, in the now. This is where our essence is revealed.

What is…it's about presence.

❧

Things To Think About

What matters now?

❧

What Is

Breath
long and deep
feels its way
through the body
choosing its
path
in and out
into the soul
out to the world
breathing the soul
out to the world
Be the soul
Breathe the soul
The soul
feels its
way through
the body
choosing its
path
in & out
into the
breath
into the world

&

It's about the breathing

It's about the breathing
The connector of all life
It's about the soft slow shallow wisp of air
into and out of our peacefulness
It's about the deep fast hard inhale into &
out of our fear
We forget to breathe sometimes
We limit our connection to all life
We limit our experience in the world
We breathe in but don't breathe out
One last breath before you go...

ॐ

90

Be the center

Be. The center.
Am I the center?
I am the requirement.
I hold the space.
I cause the space.
Be the center
Being the center
Center the being
Create the core
hold the space
let the space open
& circle
& move toward –
something.
Something bigger
greater, yet unknown…
Create the purpose
Be the purpose
invite others to become
inside the purpose
inside the being
inside the center
Am I the center?
Be the center.
Be. The center.

❧

Morning

The morning after the morning…
Awakens the soul
stirs the spirit
opens, opens, opens
receiving the gift –
Am I ready?
allowing the fullness
of spirit
to play –
to play.
to be.
to honor
to see the truth
of this space & time
we name as now
To be
To honor
To see the truth of this
space & time I name as me.

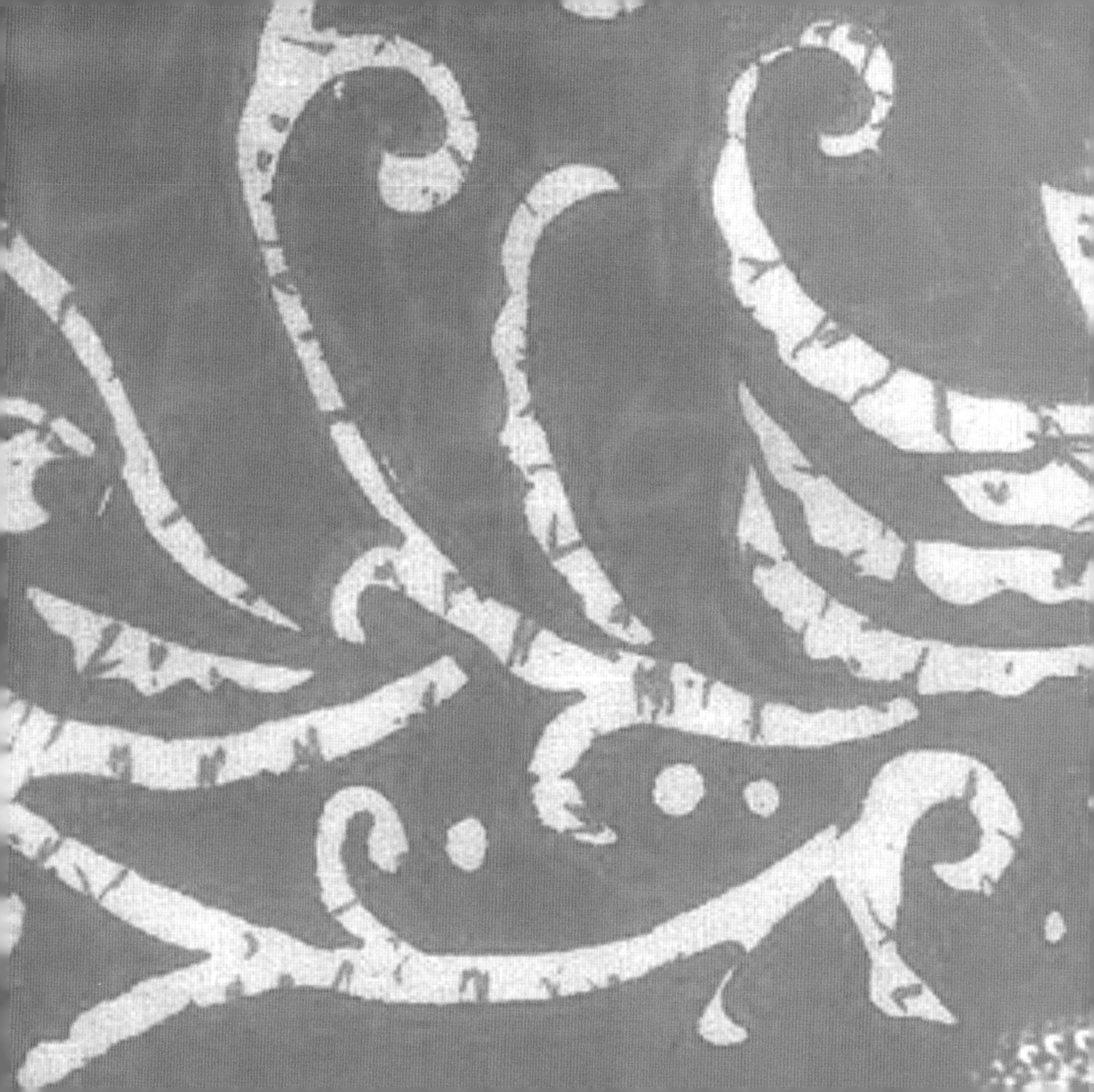

Shedding

There was time before going out on the long solo that all of us were gathered together for several days in preparation. A small cook shed is on the land for our use when we're together as a group, and for some reason I was very bothered by the clutter. There seemed this complete blindness to it – no one was dealing with it. (Perhaps they were thinking about their gear, being out there, etc., while I was trying *not* to think about my gear, being out there…) Since I'm really good at cleaning and organizing, I decided I would give the gift of renewing the cook shed. Avoidance can be very productive…

Straighten up and wipe down the counter. Well, it was much more than that. Literally, every single thing came out of that shed. Tossed, recycled, cleaned, scrubbed, swept, got new supplies. When everyone came back in from solo, they were met with a completely transformed space, a mirror of themselves.

What I didn't know at the time was how cathartic that would be for me – I playfully called the work I was doing "shedding" not realizing that I was not only shedding the shed but I was shedding a lot of what I was hanging onto around my experience of the fire the year before.

The old form is gone, taking a new shape. The butterfly is drying its wings, can no longer go back, has committed to this new life.

❧

Things To Think About

What old forms in your leadership style, your organization,
yourself, are keeping you from taking a new shape?

❧

Shedding

First the feeling
Then the question.
Then
the knowing.
What to do with
the knowing…
Be one with it
before you let it go
In denial it will
stay with you.
Say: "I see you"
And it does not
own you.
Say I see you
and the story
can be told
Say I see you
and you can
say goodbye.
Goodbye with
gratitude for
it protected
you when you needed protecting
when you craved protection from
the story you did not see.
from the feelings
you did not feel
Be one with it
and you have let
it go
Say I see you
and you have said
goodbye.

ॐ

The Spirit of Leadership

And so it is. This book is the back story, the story that happens along the way. My hope is that you let this in, that it touches you in a way that makes a difference. Because this is what leadership is really all about. The inner work we rarely hear about, the work that happens in the heart.

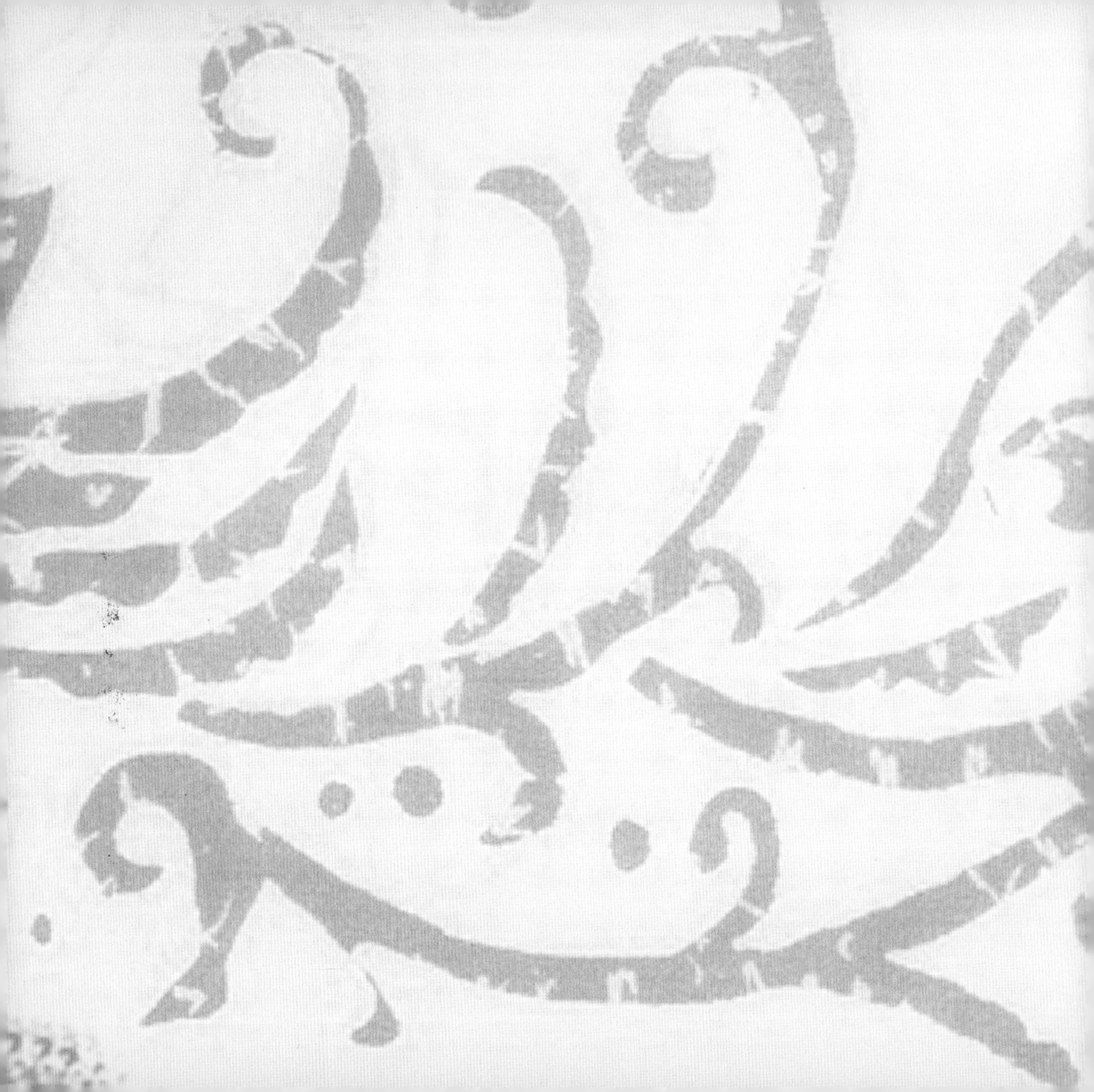

Heart 1

It's my heart, the epicenter of my energy that reverberates out out out,

touching what I may not know.

My heart fullness is my joy. I give I create I am a creator of experience,

of loving moments, of memories.

I have strength to hold all of the spirit, all of the connection, to be allowing of the flow,
to be permission for what is rarely asked for but always yearned for.

ॐ

Heart 2

It's your heart

the epicenter of the energy

that reverberates out out out,

touching what you may not know.

Your heart fullness is your joy.

You give

you create

You are a creator of experience,

of loving moments,

of memories.

You have strength to hold all of the spirit,

all of the connection,

to be allowing of the flow,

to be permission

for what is rarely asked for

but always yearned for.

&

Heart 3

ONE heart

the epicenter of the energy

that reverberates out out out,

touching what one may not know.

ONE heart fullness is one's joy.

ONE gives

ONE creates

ONE is a creator of experience,

of loving moments,

of memories.

Only ONE has strength to hold all spirit,

all connection,

to be allowing of flow,

to be permission

for what is rarely asked for

but always yearned for.

We...are ONE.

❧

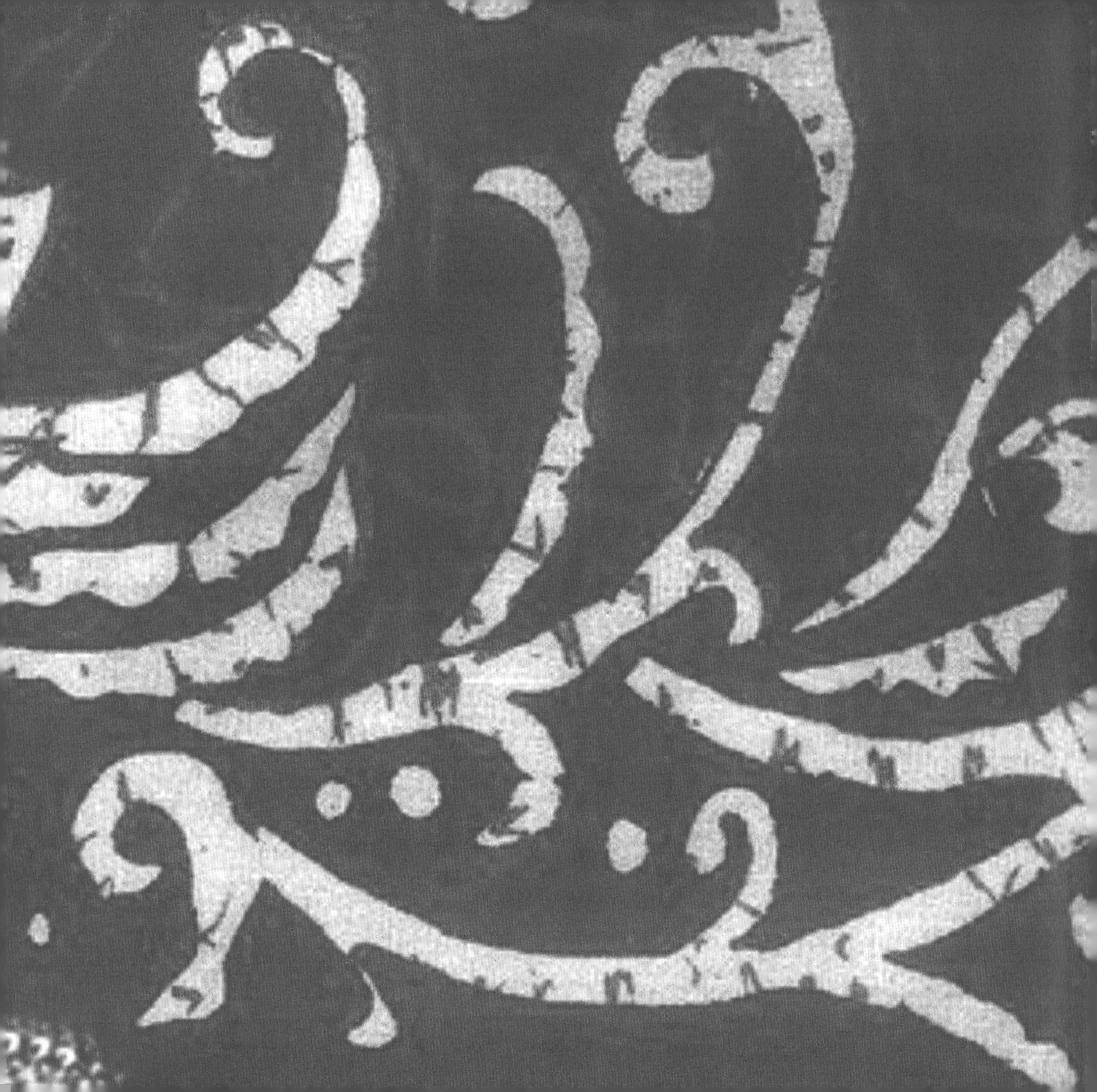

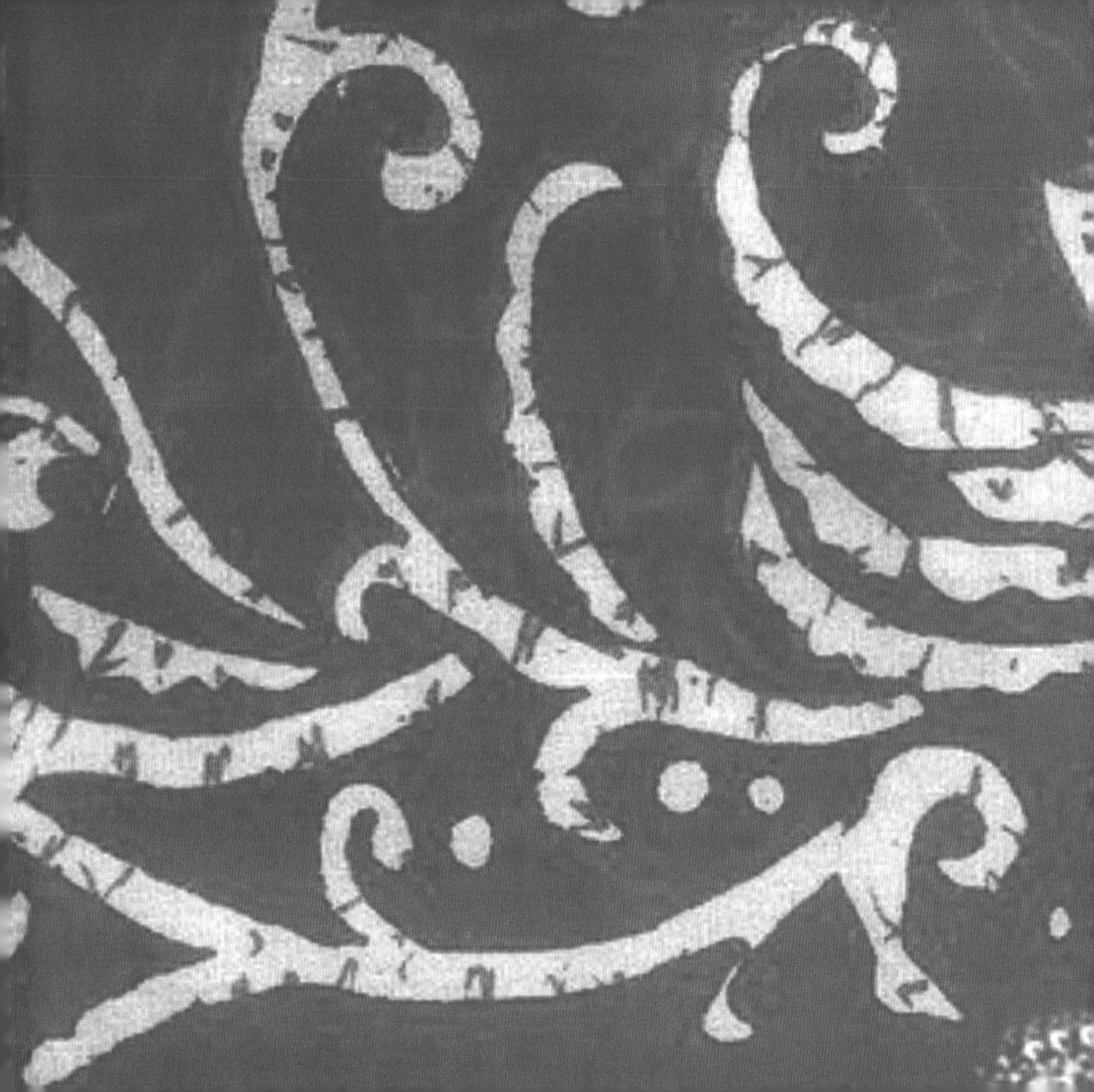

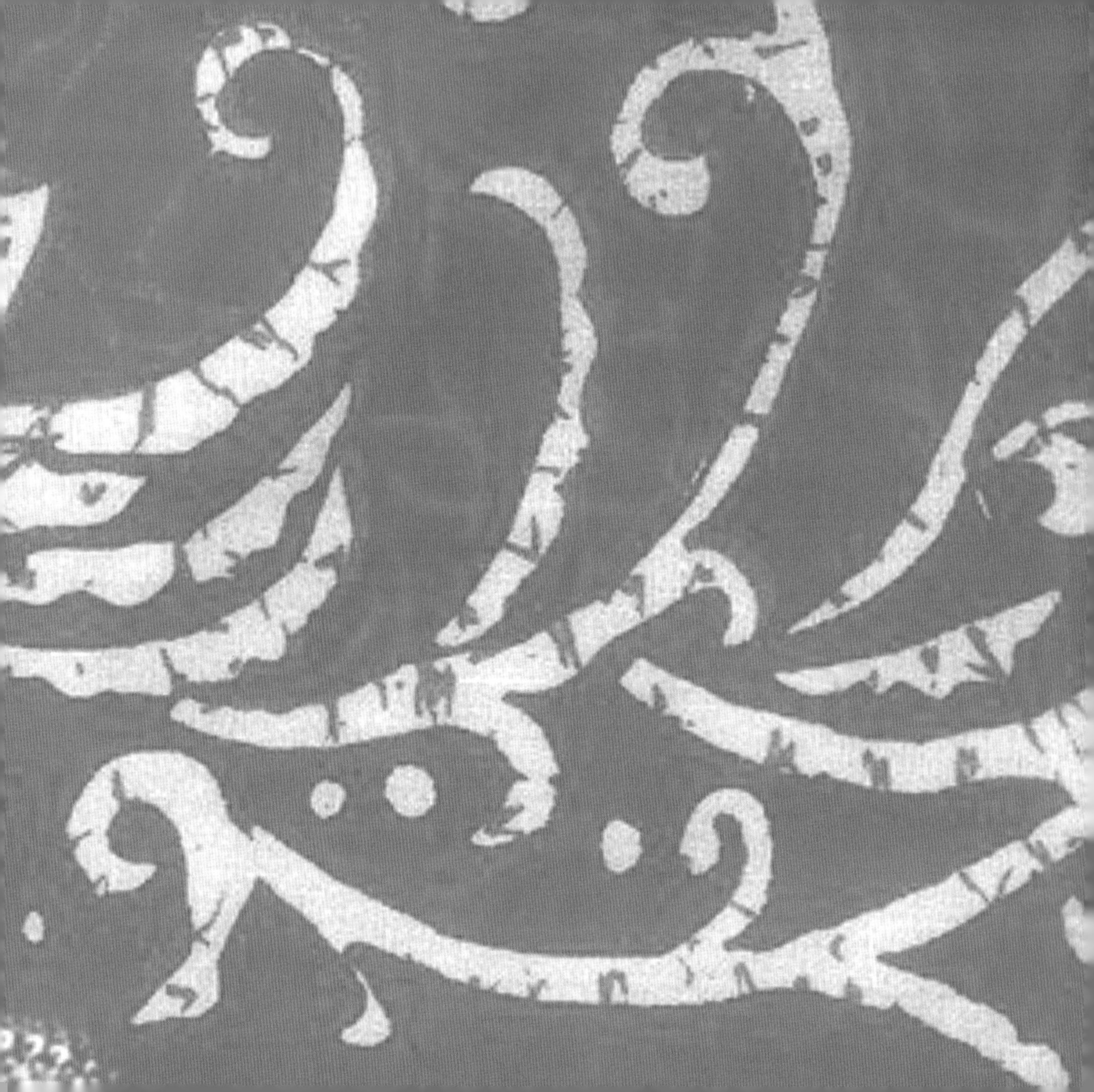

Author's Note

Throughout this book, there are references to butterflies, wilderness solos, the Way of Nature, embodied leadership.

To learn more about wilderness solos, the Way of Nature, and the teachings of John P. Milton, go to the website www.sacredpassage.com.

To learn more about embodied leadership, go to www.strozziinstitute.com.

To learn more about butterflies, visit the Museum of Natural History at the University of Florida, Gainesville, at www.flmnh.ufl.edu/butterflies.

I am indebted to ecologist Nikole Kadel for her impassioned advocacy on behalf of butterflies, their lives, their habitats, and the ecosystems that support them.

To contact Cheryl Esposito, go to www.cherylesposito.com.

❧

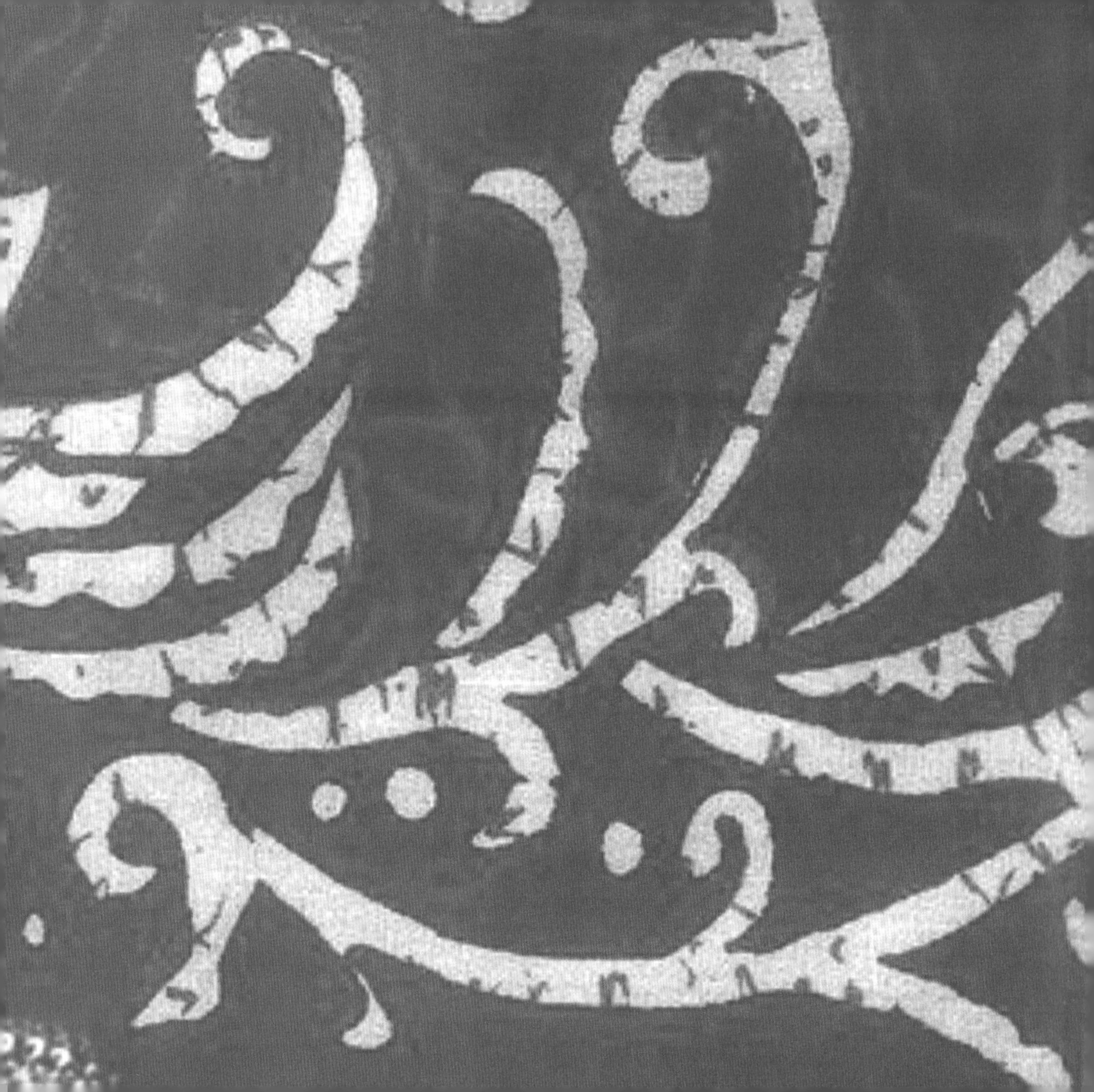

About Center for World Leadership

"Our world needs big thinkers
ideas yet to be born
thoughts nurtured into
conversations that matter"

Imagine yourself making a difference. One that others could experience; a difference that would be noticed in the world.

Now, imagine this could be anything you wanted it to be. No matter how big or small, it would be experienced by others; it would be noticed in the world.

Does this interest you? Does this inspire curiosity in you… the you who wants to play big in the world?

THE CENTER FOR WORLD LEADERSHIP creates the place for artful conversation, gathering together creative minds that are open to possible futures. Big thinkers sharing their ways of seeing so that each can bring a new found sense of possibility into the world.

Think big.. the world could become a better place because of a conversation that matters.

To learn more about Center for World Leadership, go to www.centerforworldleadership.com.